Structure and Functioning of Terrestrial Ecosystems in the Eastern Rivers and Mountains Network: Conceptual Models and Vital Signs Monitoring

Natural Resources Report NPS/NER/NRR--2006/007

James S. Rentch

Division of Forestry
West Virginia University
Morgantown, WV 26505-6125

July 2006

U.S. Department of the Interior
National Park Service
Northeast Region
Philadelphia, Pennsylvania

The Northeast Region of the National Park Service (NPS) comprises national parks and related areas in 13 New England and Mid-Atlantic states. The diversity of parks and their resources are reflected in their designations as national parks, seashores, historic sites, recreation areas, military parks, memorials, and rivers and trails. Biological, physical, and social science research results, natural resource inventory and monitoring data, scientific literature reviews, bibliographies, and proceedings of technical workshops and conferences related to these park units are disseminated through the NPS/NER Technical Report (NRTR) and Natural Resources Report (NRR) series. The reports are a continuation of series with previous acronyms of NPS/PHSO, NPS/MAR, NPS/BSO-RNR, and NPS/NERBOST. Individual parks may also disseminate information through their own report series.

Natural Resources Reports are the designated medium for information on technologies and resource management methods; "how to" resource management papers; proceedings of resource management workshops or conferences; and natural resource program descriptions and resource action plans.

Technical Reports are the designated medium for initially disseminating data and results of biological, physical, and social science research that addresses natural resource management issues; natural resource inventories and monitoring activities; scientific literature reviews; bibliographies; and peer-reviewed proceedings of technical workshops, conferences, or symposia.

Mention of trade names or commercial products does not constitute endorsement or recommendation for use by the National Park Service.

This report was accomplished under Cooperative/Interagency Acquisition Agreement H6000C02000, Task Agreement J450605720A/0003 with assistance from the NPS. The statements, findings, conclusions, recommendations, and data in this report are solely those of the author(s), and do not necessarily reflect the views of the U.S. Department of the Interior, National Park Service.

Print copies of reports in these series, produced in limited quantity and only available as long as the supply lasts, or preferably, file copies on CD, may be obtained by sending a request to the address on the back cover. Print copies also may be requested from the NPS Technical Information Center (TIC), Denver Service Center, PO Box 25287, Denver, CO 80225-0287. A copy charge may be involved. To order from TIC, refer to document D-025.

This report may also be available as a downloadable portable document format file from the Internet at http://www.nps.gov/nero/science/.

Please cite this publication as:

Rentch, James S. July 2006. Structure and functioning of Terrestrial Ecosystems in the Eastern Rivers and Mountains Network: Conceptual Models and Vital Signs Monitoring. Technical Report NPS/NER/NRR--2006/007. National Park Service. Philadelphia, PA.

NPSDNumber NPS D-025 July 2006

Table of Contents

Table of Contents (continued)

Figures

Figures (continued)

Tables

Introduction and Background

Purpose and Content of this Report

This report presents the conceptual ecological models describing the structure and function of terrestrial ecosystems for park units in the Eastern Rivers and Mountains Network (ERMN, see Table 1). These models have been developed to support the National Park Service's (NPS) Inventory and Monitoring Program (I&M Program) in this region, and in particular, to complement the identification of "vital signs" that will be used in long-term monitoring of park resources.

The report starts with background information concerning vital signs, and the physiographic and ecological scope of the report. Next, the purposes of conceptual models are discussed, and a conceptual model and literature review are presented to characterize important functional relationships among biotic and abiotic components of terrestrial ecosystems. We then summarize the main anthropogenic stressors that have caused, or threaten to cause, changes in the ecosystem integrity and sustainability, and conclude with a list of proposed vitals signs that was prepared by Hicks et al. (2005).

Vital Signs Definition

Park vital signs are selected physical, chemical, and biological elements and processes of park ecosystems that represent the overall health or condition of the park, known or hypothesized effects of stressors, or elements that have important human values. The elements and processes that are monitored are a subset of the total suite of natural resources that park managers are directed to preserve "unimpaired for future generations," including water, air, geological resources, plants and animals, and the various ecological, biological, and physical processes that act on those resources. Vital signs may occur at any level of organization including landscape, community, population, organism, or genetic level, and may be compositional (referring to the variety of elements in the system), structural (referring to the organization or pattern of the system), or functional (referring to ecological processes). For definitions, see National Park Service, http://science.nature.nps.gov/im/monitor/vsm.htm.

Goals of the I&M Vital Signs monitoring program:

- Determine status and trends in selected indicators of the condition of park ecosystems to allow managers to make better-informed decisions and to work more effectively with other agencies for the benefit of park resources.
- Provide early warning of abnormal conditions of selected resources to help develop effective mitigation measures and reduce costs of management.
- Provide data to better understand the dynamic nature and condition of park ecosystems and to provide reference points for comparisons with other altered environments.
- Provide data to meet certain legal and Congressional mandates related to natural resource protection and visitor enjoyment.
- Provide a means of measuring progress towards performance goals.

Table 1. List of parks in Eastern Rivers and Mountains (ERMN) network, with abbreviations.

ERMN Park Abbreviations	ERMN Parks
ALPO	Allegheny Portage Railroad National Historical Site
BLUE	Bluestone National Scenic River
DEWA	Delaware Water Gap National Recreational Area
FONE	Fort Necessity National Battlefield
FRHI	Friendship Hill National Historical Site
GARI	Gauley River National Recreational Area
JOFL	Johnstown Flood National Memorial
NERI	New River Gorge National River
UPDE	Upper Delaware Scenic & Recreational River

Physiographic and Ecological Scope

The geographic and physiographic extent of this report extends from the Bluestone, New, and Gauley River park complex in southern West Virginia, through the four historical parks in southwestern and central Pennsylvania, to the two Delaware River parks in northeastern Pennsylvania (Figure 1). The region is centered on the Appalachian Plateau Physiographic Province (Fenneman 1938, available at WVGES http://www.wvgs.wvnet.edu/www/geology/geolphyp.htm, and PA DCNR http://dcnr.state.pa.us/topogeo/map13/map13aspx, Figure 2).

NERI, GARI, and BLUE (see Table 1 for abbreviations) occur in the Kanawha Section of the Appalachian Plateau Physiographic Province, and FRHI is located in the Pittsburgh Low Plateau of the Kanawha Section. Here, rock formations are relatively flat, except for several distinct folds and faults on the eastern side of the Province. Local relief on the uplands is generally less than 61 m (200 ft). Local relief between valley bottoms and upland surfaces may be as much as 183 m (600 ft). Valley sides are usually moderately steep, except in the upper reaches of streams where the side slopes are fairly gentle. Elevations range from 200–520 m (660–1,700 ft). Some of the land surface in the southwestern part of the Section is very susceptible to landslides.

The oldest rocks are located in these eastern fold sequences and range in age from late Ordovician up through the Mississippian. The majority of the Appalachian Plateau is comprised of Pennsylvanian and Permian strata and is where all the minable coal is located. The rocks exposed in the northern part of the Plateau are younger than those exposed in the southern part (WVGES, http://www.wvgs.wvnet.edu/www/geology/geolphyp.htm). Stream origin is primarily fluvial erosion, and drainage patterns are dendritic. The continental climatic regime here ensures a strong annual temperature cycle, with cold winters and warm summers. Average annual temperatures range from 4–16°C (40–60°F). There is year-round precipitation, averaging from 89–152 (35–60 in) per year. Precipitation is markedly greater in the summer months when evapotranspiration is great and moisture demands are high. Only a small water deficit is incurred in summer, whereas a large surplus normally develops in spring.

The Allegheny Mountain Section lies along the eastern boundary of the plateau, and the Allegheny Front Section marks the boundary between the Appalachian Plateau Province to the west and the Ridge and Valley Physiographic Province to the east. It consists of broad, rounded ridges separated by broad valleys. The ridges decrease in elevation from south to north and the ridges have no topographic expression at the most northern end of the section. The ridges occur on the crests of anticlines that have been eroded enough to expose the very resistant rocks that form the crests of the ridges. However, not enough erosion has occurred to breach the anticlines and create parallel ridges such as occur in the Appalachian Mountain Section. These ridges form the highest mountains in Pennsylvania. The valleys are broad, undulating surfaces with shallow to deep stream incision. Relief between the ridge crests and the adjacent valley lowland can be greater than 305 m (1,000 ft). Local relief on the broad, valley lowland is generally less than 152 m (500 ft). Elevations in the Section range from 236–979 m (775–3,213 ft).

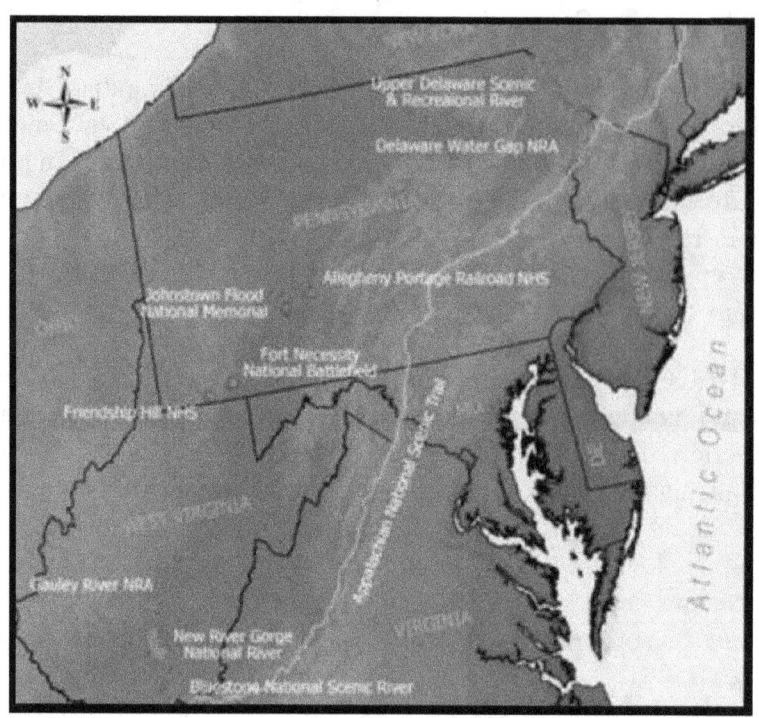

Figure 1. Location map of member parks of Eastern Rivers and Mountains Network (ERMN)

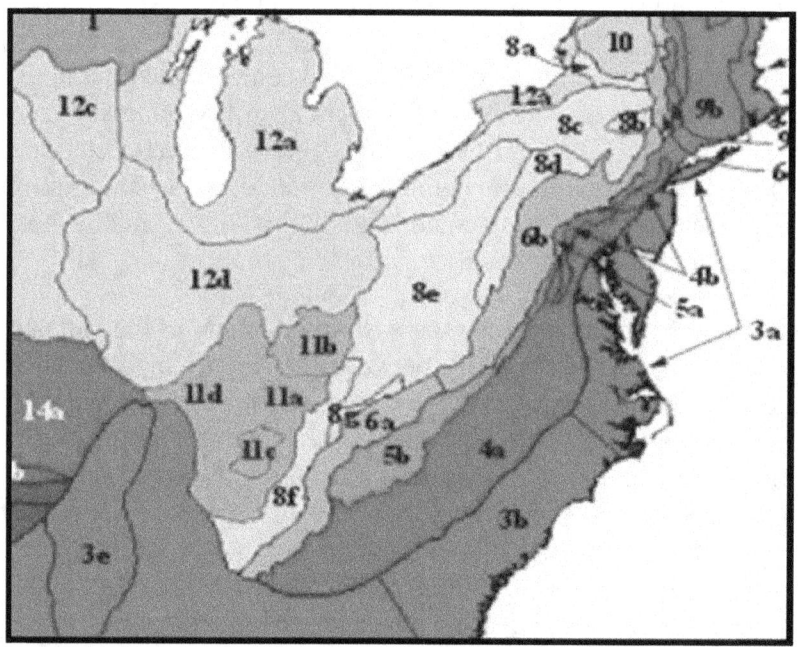

Figure 2. Physical Divisions of the United States, U.S. Geological Survey (Fenneman 1946). Areas labeled 8a-e are the Appalachian Plateau Physiographic Province. Areas labeled 6a-b are the Ridge and Valley Province.

DEWA and UPDE occur in the Glaciated Low Plateau Section of the Appalachian Physiographic Province, which includes an area of diversified topography in northeastern Pennsylvania. The topography consists of rounded hills and broad to narrow valleys all of which have been modified by glacial erosion and deposition. Swamps and peat bogs are common in the eastern part of the Section. The Section reflects the interplay between bedrock of various types, mainly sandstones and siltstones, and glacial erosion and deposition. The more erosion-resistant rocks form the hills, while the less erosion-resistant rocks occur in the valleys. Glacial deposits, mainly glacial till or sand and gravel, may occur anywhere, but are found mainly in the valley bottoms and margins.

The climate is temperate, with distinct summer and winter, and all areas are subject to frost. Average annual temperatures range from below 10°C (50°F) in the north to about 18°C (64°F) at the south end of the highlands. The average length of the frost-free period is about 100 days in the northern mountains, and about 220 days in the low southern parts of the Appalachian Highlands. Average annual precipitation varies from 89 cm (35 in) the valleys to up to 203 cm (80 in) on the highest peaks—the highest in the Eastern United States. Precipitation is fairly well distributed throughout the year. Snowfall is more than 61 cm (24 in) in Pennsylvania, increasing southward along the mountains. South-facing slopes are notably warmer and drier than north-facing slopes, and one result is that forest fires are more frequent on south-facing slopes.

The Nature Conservancy (TNC) has delineated five ecoregions that encompass the ERMN area (Figure 3, TNC 2000a). Ecoregions are large units on the landscape; following are summary descriptions of ecoregions as they apply to ERMN units. Note that the description of the Western Allegheny Plateau, which includes FRHI, is not available, although this park lies on the western edge of the Central Appalachians Ecoregion.

NERI and GARI are included in the Cumberland Mountains subregion of the Cumberlands and Southern Ridge and Valley Ecoregion (CSRV). The CSRV is a highly variable landscape with a complex geologic history. The Cumberland Mountains subregion is comprised of a high plateau and low mountains, and landforms are the product of differential weathering of the Pennsylvanian Period sandstone (WVGES, available at http://www.wvgs.wvnet.edu/www/geology/geoles01.htm). The climate of the region is temperate and mild with favorable growing conditions. The physical parameters of the region are variable; however, the general range of gradients has resulted in a multitude of habitats for species and natural plant communities. Major habitats range from broad river floodplains to small, ephemeral streams, high mountains to deep gorges, and dry barrens and to mesic forests (TNC 2003). Smaller scale habitats such as caves, cliffs, flatrock river scour communities, and xeric, rimrock pine communities also contribute to habitat and species diversity (see Mahan 2004).

Ecologically, the ecoregion is known for high biological diversity, endemism, and species rareness. In the region, the US Fish and Wildlife Service identified 248 species and subspecies as endangered, threatened, or candidates for listing. Over 544 conservation targets were selected by TNC during development of its conservation plan for the region. Targets include 364 animal and plant species and 180 natural plant communities and ecological systems (TNC 2003). The high level of rarity/diversity and conservation values can be attributed to a number of factors.

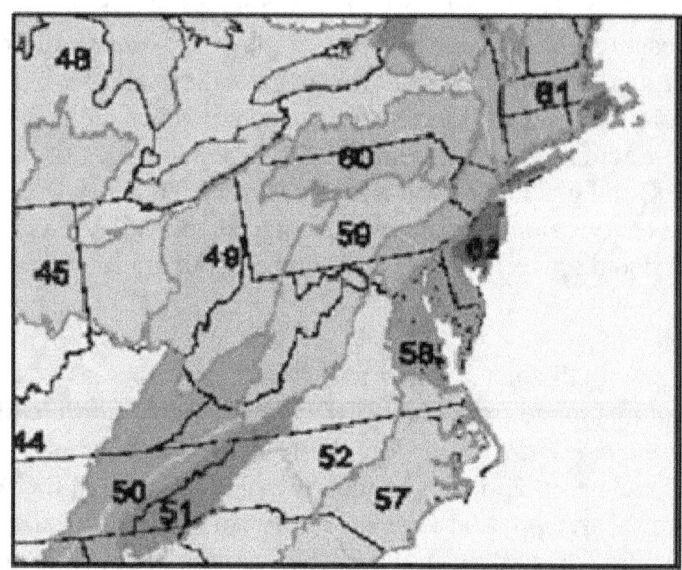

Figure 3. Ecoregions of the eastern United States. Ecoregion 50 = Cumberlands and Southern Ridge and Valley, 49 = Western Allegheny Plateau, 59 = Central Appalachians, 60 = High Allegheny Plateau, and 61 = Lower New England-Southern Piedmont (modified from TNC 2000a).

The region escaped glaciation, and the north–south orientation of the mountains and valleys facilitated species retreat southward ahead of the ice sheets, and advance northward as the ice sheets retreated (Delcourt and Delcourt 1987, 1998; Bonnicker 2000). This region, and in particular, the New River, became a migratory crossroads for northern and southern species. Core (1966) and Strausbaugh and Core (1977) identified eight southern plant species that migrated north into West Virginia along the New and Potomac Rivers. One of these (*Halesia carolina*) occurs no further north than NERI.

ALPO, JOFL, FONE, and BLUE all occur in the Central Appalachian Forest Ecoregion. This ecoregion includes the Blue Ridge Mountains, the Great Valley, and portions of the Allegheny Mountains that stretch southwest to northeast. This assemblage provides unique and significant contributions to biological diversity of eastern North America. It is a center of endemism for several biotic groups, including 12 vascular plants of shale barren communities, dozens of species endemic to subterranean habitats, and a number of plants, invertebrates, salamanders, and small mammals. It also includes clusters of significantly disjunct species. Biodiversity is high because the region was completely unglaciated, and the region contains some of the highest environmental diversity in eastern North America. Annual precipitation ranges from 76–216 cm (30–85 in), much of which is snow. The region contains some of the highest summits in the east, and the greatest amount of land higher than 792 m (2,600 ft), outside the southern Blue Ridge. There is, as well, substantial geologic variation including sedimentary shales, limestones, and sandstones, and igneous basalt (TNC 2001). In the ecoregion conservation plan, TNC identified 74 plant, 30 vertebrate, and 110 invertebrate species for conservation within the region. In addition, 142 terrestrial and palustrine communities were also targeted.

Parks along the Delaware River in eastern Pennsylvania are part of the Lower New England-Northern Piedmont Ecoregion (DEWA), and the High Allegheny Plateau Ecoregion (DEWA and UPDE). The High Allegheny Plateau Ecoregion has the highest percentage of natural cover (86%) of any northeastern ecoregion except the Northern Appalachian Ecoregion. Forest cover is primarily deciduous (52%) and mixed deciduous-coniferous (21%). Coniferous forest covers only 6%, however a significant portion of hemlock (*Tsuga canadensis*) resources occurs in this ecoregion, particularly in riparian zones. All of the ecoregion is influenced by major rivers. The upper drainages of the Delaware River originate within the region and drain the west and south slopes of the Catskill Mountains. Much of the region has been glaciated, and features on the landscape include end moraine, eskers, drumlins, kettleholes, and other features associated with the terminus of the ice sheet advance and deposits associated with glacial meltwater flow. One of the main features of the ecoregion is its low population density, although major population centers are nearby. Regionwide, the overall population trend is decline, however several areas, particularly in the Poconos, have become centers of first- and second-home development.

The climate of the ecoregion is characteristic of high elevation areas in the mid-Atlantic region: hot, humid summers and cold winters with moderate snowfall. Also characteristic are periodic droughts that occur principally in the summer months. These can have profound effects on vegetation and aquatic systems, particularly when under additional biotic or abiotic stresses. The dominant vegetation is beech-maple forests at lower elevation mesic sites, and Appalachian oak on drier sites; oak-hickory forests occupy many south-facing, dry slopes, and in the eastern part of the region, pine barrens occur on rocky ridges. The Nature Conservancy identified 109 vegetation types (TNC 2004). Conservation targets for this ecoregion include 72 priority aquatic units, 253 natural community occurrences, 74 animals, and 88 plants.

The eastern edge of UPDE also abuts the Lower New England Ecoregion. An Ecological Land Use analysis of this region identified 486 biophysical combinations of a potential 630 combinations based on lithology, topography, and elevation (TNC 2000b). Absent field data, this suggests considerable biologic diversity as well. A number of endemic species occur here, and the region's long north–south axis captures species and natural communities more representative of the Northern Appalachian/Boreal ecoregions at higher elevations, and southern species in the Piedmont. Primary conservation targets identified by TNC include eight vertebrates, 57 invertebrates, and 42 plant species.

Narrative of Structural and Functional Relationship : A Conceptual Model

Introduction

A conceptual model is a purposeful representation of reality that provides a mental picture of how something works to communicate that explanation to others. The conceptual ecological model we present is a visual and/or narrative summary that summarizes the important components of the ecosystem and the interactions among them. Models show how natural drivers (e.g. climate) and anthropogenic stressors (e.g. climate change) affect ecosystem function and aid in interpreting trends in these vital signs against the backdrop of their long-term natural variation. Development of a conceptual model helps in understanding how the diverse components of a monitoring program interact, and promotes integration and communication among scientists and managers from different disciplines. Useful conceptual models, therefore, do all or most of the following:

- articulate important processes and variables.
- contribute to understanding interactions between ecosystem processes and dynamics.
- identify key links between drivers, stressors, and system responses.
- facilitate selection and justification of monitoring variables.
- facilitate evaluation of data from the monitoring program.
- facilitate communication of processes among scientists and program staff, between scientists and managers, and with the general public.

Background: the Jenny-Chapin Model

Jenny (1941, 1980) and Chapin et al. (1996) proposed that a sustainable ecosystem is one that, over the normal cycle of disturbance events (i.e., decades to centuries), maintains its characteristic diversity of major functional groups, productivity, soil fertility, and rates of biogeochemical cycling. Ecosystem properties are governed by internal interactions and external factors. Five independent external *state factors* (parent material, climate, topography, potential biota, and time since disturbance) determine limits of ecosystem processes. These state factors are, in turn, modified by a set of four dynamic, *interactive controls*: local/regional climate, soil resource supply, major functional groups of organisms, and disturbance regime (see Figure 4). In contrast to state factors, interactive controls both control and respond to ecosystem characteristics; they are both constrained by state factors and respond to ecosystem processes (Chapin et al. 1996).

For example, regional climate is affected not only by solar input and moisture supplies from oceans, but also by forest cover (e.g., functional groups), which determines the amount of energy that is absorbed by the ecosystem and is available to heat the atmosphere (Chapin and Whiteman 1998). Soil resources are affected not only by the parent material, but also by the chemical composition and decomposition rates of leaf litter produced by plants (Hobbie 1992), and by the extent of browsing by herbivores (Pastor et al. 1988). Nutrient supply then determines the relative abundance of forest types, which affect fire return time. Human activities also influence forest composition through harvest management decisions and business strategies of forest industries; forest composition, in turn, affects fire probability (Starfield and Chapin 1996),

9

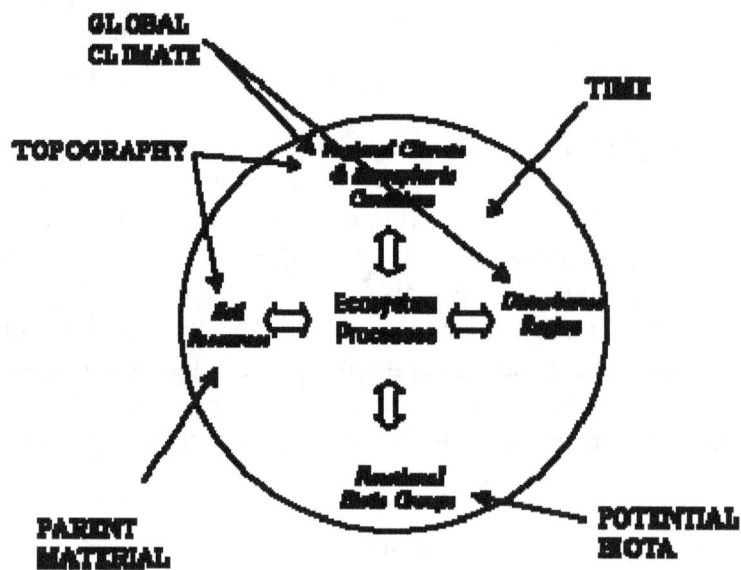

Figure 4. Chapin et al. (1996) ecosystem model of relationship between state factors, interactive controls, and ecosystem processes. State factors are capitalized; interactive controls are underlined, and the circle represents the boundary of the ecosystem.

nutrient cycling rates (Hobbie 1992), and regional climate (Foley et al. 1994). In summary, the major factors that determine the structure and functioning of ecosystems are also strongly affected by ecosystem processes and their interactions with human activities.

For vital signs monitoring, a key component of the Jenny-Chapin framework is the principle that interactive controls must be conserved if an ecosystem is to be maintained, and that major changes in any interactive control will result in a new ecosystem with distinctly different properties. Thus for example, a change in the natural fire regime may result in altered light resources on the forest floor, changes in a species' reproductive success, a realignment of competitive relationships between plant species and species groups in a forest community, and thus compositional and structural changes in plant communities (e.g., Abrams 1992) and rates of biogeochemical cycling. Similarly, alteration of soil resources as a result of acid precipitation may change the mycorrhizal community composition, which in turn may affect vegetative germination and growth rates, species presence/absence, and the rates of natural forest development (e.g., Blaney and Miller 1995).

General Model—Ecosystem Processes

Key ecosystem processes include geophysical, biological, and ecological components.

Geophysical Processes

Geophysical processes include land cover, land use, and landscape patterns. Across a landscape, habitat diversity, connectivity, isolation, and landscape change are important components of the geophysical setting. Soil composition and chemistry, and the rate of weathering of parent material, and water quality all determine site productivity and quality.

Biological Processes

Biological processes are defined by compositional and structural characteristics of the biota on the individual, community, and landscape level. Taxonomic composition, fecundity, growth, health, vigor, and survival and mortality are components. Key indicators of a healthy and sustainable biota are biodiversity and compositional resilience, including both rare species and invasive species populations.

Ecological Processes

Ecological processes include those that cycle energy and materials through the system—the biogeochemical links between organisms and their environment. Primary productivity, nutrient cycling, water cycling, decomposition and mineralization, and food webs are key ecological processes.

General Model—Interactive Controls

Using the Jenny-Chapin model, we review the four interactive controls (climate, weather, and atmospheric conditions, disturbance regimes, major functional biotic groups, and soil resources and conditions) for the ERMN terrestrial systems identified in Figures 2 and 3.

Regional Climate

On broad geographic scales, climate is the interactive control that most strongly governs the structure, productivity, and biogeochemistry of ecosystems (Chapin et al. 1996). Climate affects genetic differentiation and speciation (Barnes 1991), species migrations, distributions and associations (Braun 1950; Watts 1979; Davis 1981; Iverson et al. 1999), competition (Abrams 1998), disturbance regimes (Dale et al. 2001; Schoennagel et al. 2004), as well as growth rates and carbon balance (Anderson 1991; Aber et al. 2001; McGuire et al. 2001). Temperature and precipitation patterns, as they interact with vegetation, parent materials, and topography, are important in determining soils processes and soil development (Barnes et al. 1998). Finally, climate and climate change also have important economic and socioeconomic impacts, including consumption of forest products and recreation services (Irland et al. 2001).

A summary of normal precipitation and temperature trends for the past 30 years from stations within the ERMN region shows a slight latitudinal gradient with regard to average monthly precipitation and temperature (Table 2, Figure 5). Northernmost parks tend to have colder and wetter falls and winters; however, differences during the growing season are much less in magnitude. In the region covered in this report, precipitation is well distributed throughout the growing season and is generally not limiting to growth, except on the most drought-prone sites such as pine flats, clifftops, and talus slopes. Droughts occur, however, drought effects in eastern mesic forests have been shown to last for only 2 to 3 years (Cook and Jacoby 1977; Jacobi and Tainter 1988; Orwig and Abrams 1997), and sustained growth declines (approx. five years or more) associated with drought are observed for only the most severe drought events (Rubino and McCarthy 2000). Instead, the forests of the ERMN are characterized by a relatively high degree of climatic complacency. That is, over decadal time scales, tree growth patterns show relatively low variability, indicating that tree growth is less affected by variations in climate (Fritts 1976) than by the effects of canopy disturbance and competition between plant organisms for growing space (Phipps 1982; Nowacki and Abrams 1997; Rentch et al. 2002).

While most evidence supports our assertion that inter-annual variability in climate is the dominant climatic signal in eastern mesic forests, there is some evidence that longer-term climatic trends may be present. Long-term, non-periodic trends, such as global warming, for example, may increase drought frequency (LeBlanc and Foster 1992) and alter species distributions (Iverson et al. 1999). In addition, the North Atlantic Oscillation is an intermittent climate oscillation with temporally active and passive phases. Periods of 5–7, 9–11, 12–14, and 80–90 years have been identified (Appenzeller and Stocker 1998). Although this phenomenon has been primarily linked to winter climate and phenology of herbaceous plants in Europe (Post and Stenseth 1999; Otterson et al. 2001), research in North America suggests an impact here as well. For example, McCabe et al. (2004) attributed more than half (52%) of the spatial and temporal variance in multi-decadal drought frequency over the lower 48 states to the Pacific Decadal Oscillation (PDO) and the Atlantic Multidecadal Oscillation (AMO), and that much of the long-term predictability of drought frequency resided in the multidecadal behavior of the North Atlantic Ocean.

Table 2. Mean monthly temperature normals (F) and precipitation (in) from weather stations near ERMN facilities (1971–2001) (NCDC 2005).

Temperature Normals	Jan	Feb	Mar	Apr	May	Jun	Jul	Aug	Sep	Oct	Nov	Dec	Year
Bluestone Lake (BLUE)	31.2	34.8	43.1	52.3	61.0	69.1	73.3	72.3	66.0	54.4	44.0	34.6	53.0
Summersville Lake (GARI)	28.8	31.5	39.7	49.4	58.7	66.5	70.5	69.0	63.1	51.8	42.3	33.4	50.4
Morgantown Lock and Dam (FRHI, FONE)	30.8	33.7	42.6	52.3	61.3	69.4	73.5	72.1	65.8	54.4	44.3	35.4	53.0
Johnstown (JOFL)	29.2	32.0	40.5	51.7	61.4	69.9	73.9	72.0	65.1	53.2	43.6	33.6	52.2
Altoona (ALPO)	26.5	29.1	37.5	48.9	59.0	67.2	71.1	69.8	63.3	51.9	42.1	31.5	49.8
Stroudsburg (DEWA, UPDE)	25.8	27.8	37.5	48.8	58.8	67.3	71.9	70.2	62.1	50.7	40.3	30.9	49.3
Precipitation Normals	Jan	Feb	Mar	Apr	May	Jun	Jul	Aug	Sep	Oct	Nov	Dec	Year
Bluestone Lake (BLUE)	3.0	2.7	3.5	3.3	4.0	3.3	4.2	3.3	2.8	2.6	2.5	2.6	37.8
Summersville Lake (GARI)	3.6	3.1	3.9	3.8	4.8	4.4	5.5	4.7	3.6	3.3	3.3	3.5	47.5
Morgantown Lock and Dam (FRHI, FONE)	3.3	2.9	3.8	3.7	4.4	4.0	4.2	4.0	3.4	2.9	3.5	3.3	43.4
Johnstown (JOFL)	3.8	3.4	3.9	3.8	4.3	4.9	5.1	4.1	4.2	3.3	3.7	3.3	47.8
Altoona (ALPO)	2.8	2.6	3.6	3.7	4.4	4.3	4.0	3.3	4.0	3.4	3.7	2.9	42.7
Stroudsburg (DEWA, UPDE)	4.0	3.0	3.8	4.0	5.0	4.6	4.4	4.3	4.9	3.8	4.3	3.9	50.0

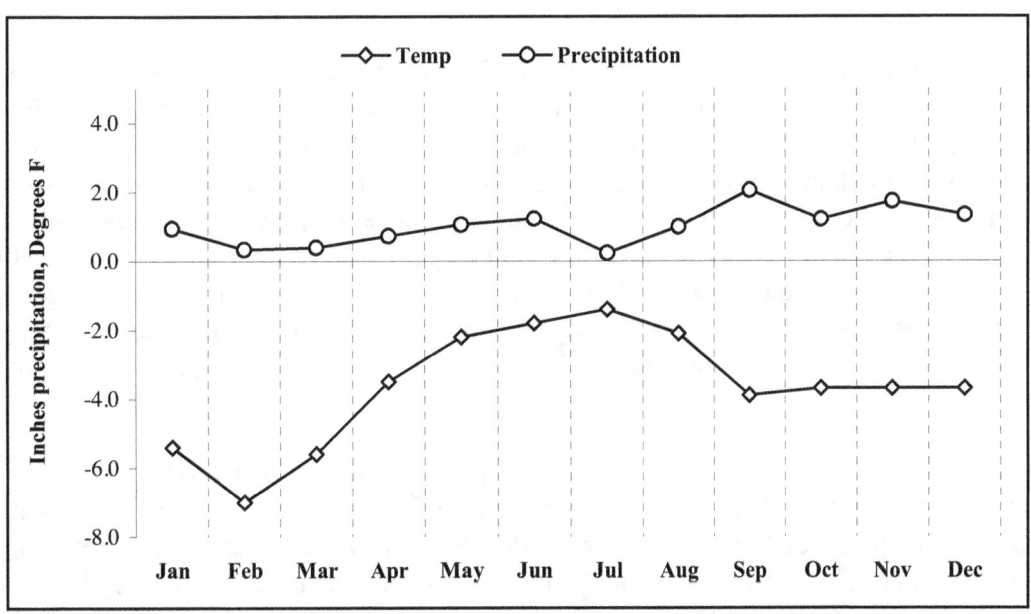

Figure 5. Differences in mean monthly precipitation and temperature normals for northernmost (UPDE) and southernmost (BLUE) ERMN facilities, using data from weather stations near ERMN facilities, 1971–2000 (USCDC 2005.

13

Natural Disturbance Regime

Pickett and White (1985) defined disturbance as "any relatively discrete event in time that disrupts ecosystem, community, or population structure, and changes resources, substrate availability, or the physical environment." Oliver and Larsen (1996) focused on vegetation dynamics: "disturbances kill vegetation and release growing space." Disturbance regimes, on the other hand, consist of all the disturbances that affect an area (Runkle 1985), the pattern of death of dominant individuals (canopy trees) in a community (Runkle 1982), and the temporal and spatial pattern of creation of open or altered spaces (Pickett and White 1985).

Descriptors of natural disturbance regimes include the following: 1) spatial distribution (where disturbances occur on the landscape); 2) temporal distribution (how often do they occur), expressed as disturbance frequency (f), return interval (= 1/f), or rotation (= f x area); 3) size (ha); 4) predictability (the variance of the return interval, related to historic range of variability); 5) magnitude—intensity (the physical force/unit of area or time, and severity [impacts on organisms, communities, and ecosystems])—these may occur along gradient from major or severe to minor; major disturbances or stand-replacing events kill from the bottom up, usually with alteration in soil resources, while minor disturbances kill from top down, usually leaving residuals in lower layers as successors; and 6) synergism and feedbacks are interactions of one disturbance or chronic stress on others—for example, drought may increase the probability of fire or insect outbreak, a light surface fire that consumes coarse woody debris and kills understory stems may make reduce the probability of an intense crown fire, or a hurricane-size blowdown may increase the probability of fire (Pickett and White 1985; Oliver and Larsen 1996).

Disturbances are spatially and temporally patchy (Runkle 1985) and they occur on a variety of spatial and temporal scales. These range from single-tree canopy gaps to catastrophic fire to climate change and glacial removal. At the landscape level, the combination of small, medium-sized, and large disturbances tends to create a mosaic of patches of varying size, species, and structure, and this patchiness affects levels of resource availability, survival of residuals, and rate of invasion and successful re-establishment. Frequency and return interval, expressions of temporal variability, have enormous biological significance. They may have as strong a selective effect on species composition as physical characteristics of the environment (Denslow 1980, 1985), because they tell us which species can inhabit an ecosystem for long periods of time.

Disturbances affect many levels of biological organization and produce variability in composition and structure. They can either reinitiate early stages of stand development (e.g., a stand-initiating disturbance [Oliver and Larsen 1996]), or they may accelerate succession (e.g., disturbance-mediated succession [Abrams and Scott 1989]). Disturbances overlay environmental gradients, both influencing and being influenced by those gradients. For example, fires are more likely and burn more intensely on drier terrain than moister terrain. Guyette and Dey (2000) found that 50% variance of fire frequency was accounted for by "topographic roughness" in one watershed in Missouri (1700–1750). Conversely, some disturbances (e.g., hurricanes) are largely independent of physical gradients.

Finally, disturbances interact (Sousa 1984; White et al. 1999). Windthrow may increase the likelihood of fire; fire decreases the likelihood of windthrow. Disturbances are usually thought of as being allogenic phenomena—phenomena not generated by changes within the stand. However, they are partly autogenic, since the impact of disturbance is the result of both the magnitude of the disturbance, and the predisposition of the stand to the particular disturbance type (Oliver and Larsen 1996). As forests age, they may become more susceptible to disturbance; thus, the magnitude of disturbance required to disrupt the stand becomes less with age. For example, windthrow becomes more likely when trees are taller.

Disturbance-driven spatial and temporal variability is a vital attribute of all ecosystems. For the purposes of vital signs monitoring and ecosystem sustainability, disturbances are considered to be interactive controls if they fall within the historical range of natural variability (HRV) of an ecosystem. Morgan et al.'s (1994) definition of natural variability reflects this distinction: fluctuations in ecosystem conditions or processes over time, [defined by] the bounds of system behavior that remain relatively consistent over time. Landres et al.'s (1999) definition is similar: "the ecological conditions and spatial and temporal variation in these conditions that are relatively unaffected by people, within a period of time and geographical area appropriate to an expressed goal." Disturbances that are described by these concepts should be differentiated from stressors, which may meet the strict definition of disturbance (i.e., kill trees and release growing space), but fall outside the historic range of natural variability of the ecosystem. Ecosystem stressors are physical, chemical, or biological perturbations to a system that are either a) foreign to that system, or b) natural to the system but applied at excessive (or deficient) levels (Barrett et al. 1976).

An important methodological question revolves around the need to identify an appropriate time period and spatial extent used in defining natural variation for any ecosystem. This includes a consideration of the influence of people. Many applications of natural variability consider the time before Euro-American settlement as that during which the natural environment was "relatively unaffected by people" (Hunter 1996). However, current research is accumulating data that suggests that native-American populations had considerable influence over the natural environment (see e.g., Delcourt 1987; Delcourt and Delcourt 1998; Bonnicksen 2000). Conversely, Vail (1998) criticizes the "myth of the humanized environment" and suggests that, for many areas, the influence of native-Americans has been overstated. Landres et al. (1999) notes that use of natural variability always depends on the ecological and social context, and that selection of appropriate time period and area should be guided by specific goals, objectives, assumptions, and value judgments, as well as data availability and quality.

In eastern, mesic, deciduous forests of the type found in ERMN units, most forest turnover is associated with small, single- and multiple-tree canopy gaps (Runkle 1982, 1990). Major, stand-initiating disturbances reach perhaps their lowest level of importance for forest types in the eastern United States (Runkle 1990). Tornadoes occur, but are relatively rare. The frequency of large-scale wind events declines in the southern portion of ERMN (Runkle 1982, 1985, 1990). Wind is the dominant agent of gap formation (Barden 1981; Romme and Martin 1982; Runkle 1985; Clebsch and Busing 1989) and single and multiple tree-fall gaps are the dominant disturbance type (Runkle 1982; Crow 1988), especially as forests mature. Winds and thunderstorms accounted for 40–70% of severe weather events in portions of WV and southwestern PA in one study (Rentch 2003a). In a study that examined five oak-dominated stands in three states, small-scale disturbances occurred, on average, every three years, while larger events, involving more than one tree, occur on a 17-year interval (Rentch et al. 2003a). While wind is the most common precipitating cause, excessive rainfall, flooding, erosion and soil slippage, insect defoliation and/or fungal infestation, lightning strike, drought, and many others may be contributing factors.

As a canopy disturbance, fire is more important around the edges of the region in the coniferous forests of the southeast, west, and north (Frost 1998; Duchesne 2000; Wade et al. 2000). In the Appalachian Plateau, however, a highly dissected topography with frequent natural firebreaks limits the size of potential fire compartments (Frost 1998). Lightning is an occasional ignition source, particularly during drought years (Ruffner and Abrams 1998), but low correlations between climate and fire frequency suggest that most fires in this region are caused by humans (Sutherland 1997; Wade et al. 2000). Fires most often occur on the forest floor in the dormant season (Sutherland 1997). This, in addition to the absence of fuel accumulation, means that the immediate effects of fires in the region are largely concentrated in the understory (see Figure 6).

Although there are relatively few long-term fire chronologies for this region, there is a growing consensus that human use (and misuse) of fire has had a significant impact on forest composition and structure. Prior to European settlement, fire was a significant component of the disturbance regime, and strongly correlated with native-American habitation and land-use patterns (Delcourt and Delcourt 1987, 1998; Bonnicksen 2000). These were primarily low-intensity ground fires (i.e., "the Indian way," Pyne 2001) during the dormant season. Fire return intervals as low as two years (McCarthy et al. 2001) and eight years (Buell et al. 1954; Abrams 2000) have been reported. During the 1800s, European settlers used fire for many of the same reasons as native-Americans, and fire frequencies remained the same or increased (Van Lear and Waldrop 1989; Sutherland 1997; Abrams 2000; Wade et al. 2000). Since 1900, a fire suppression policy has greatly reduced fire frequency and the annual area burned (Abrams 1992; Wade et al. 2000). This has resulted in altered patterns of species competition, regeneration, and canopy accession, particularly for oaks species (Abrams 1992; Rentch et al. 2003b). Additional endangered community-types in the ERMN that are known to be fire-maintained are rimrock pine communities of Virginia and pitch pine. These occur along exposed cliffs in the New River and Delaware River parks, and are thought to have been maintained by periodic fires burning up the slopes of the gorge (Brose and Waldrop 2000; Vanderhorst 2002; Waldrop et al. 2003; Mahan 2004).

Soil Resources

All terrestrial vegetation requires five primary resources for growth and development: light, CO_2, water, mineral nutrients, and a porous media for physical rooting and support (Barnes et al. 1998). Although plants obtain light from solar radiation and CO_2 from the atmosphere, the remaining resources are provided by soil. In turn, the rate of weathering of parent material and soil development are strongly modified by biota, particularly through carbonation weathering and the production of organic acids in the upper soil profile (Schlesinger 1997). Soil resources determine the maximum potential productivity and structural diversity of vegetation, and ultimately, the entire biota (Chapin et al. 1996).

16

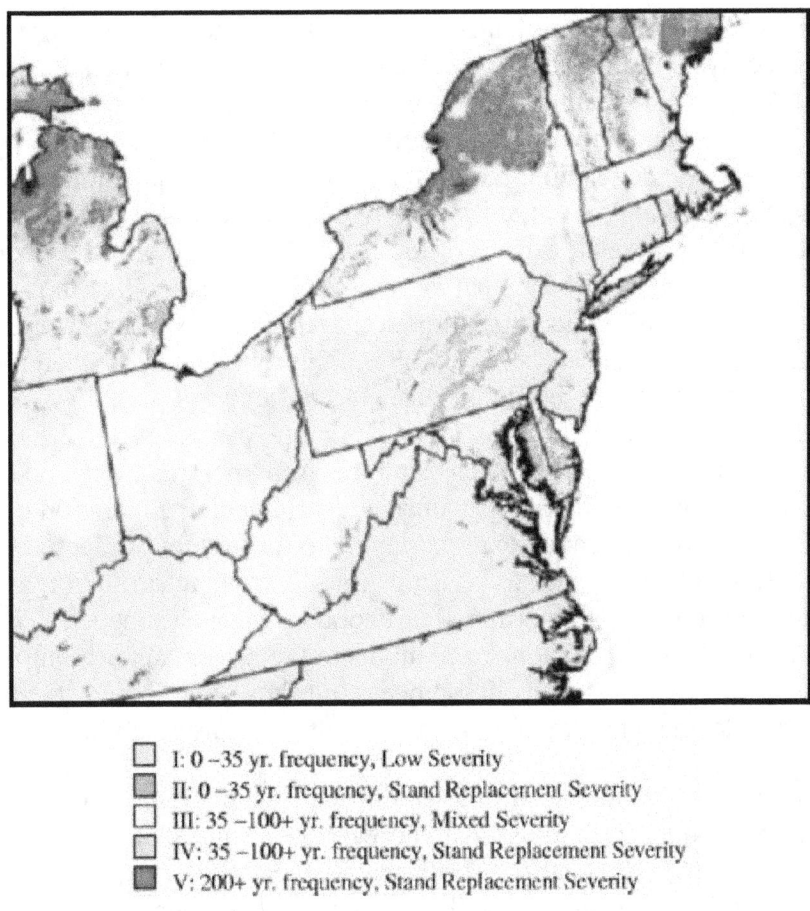

I: 0 – 35 yr. frequency, Low Severity
II: 0 – 35 yr. frequency, Stand Replacement Severity
III: 35 – 100+ yr. frequency, Mixed Severity
IV: 35 – 100+ yr. frequency, Stand Replacement Severity
V: 200+ yr. frequency, Stand Replacement Severity

Figure 6. Fire regime map of the United States, showing fire frequency and intensity (from Schmidt et al. 2002).

The biogeochemical cycling of mineral nutrients is one of the most important processes occurring in forest ecosystems, and temperate deciduous forests are remarkably conservative and efficient systems. Waring and Running (1998) summarized the processes involved both within (in the soil/plant interface) and without (in the atmosphere and export [Figure 7]). Soil nutrients are supplied by atmospheric deposition, fixation, and weathering of parent material. Plants take up nutrients during the growing season, utilize them in plant processes such as photosynthesis, and metabolize them into a variety of forms of biomass. Some nutrients are sequestered into wood and root tissue, but much of the annual nutrient uptake is returned to the system as leaf detritus and woody debris, where decomposition eventually releases it in forms that are again available for uptake by plant roots and soil microbes. Nutrient cycling is, therefore, a pattern of fluxes in the system—the processes of uptake, use, and reuse over time. It is a seasonally regulated process driven by phenological variations in biotic processes that are themselves regulated by cyclical climatic processes, such as temperature, precipitation, and solar radiation (Hicks et al. 1992). Because of intra-system nutrient cycling and the retention of past inputs, plant growth is not solely dependent on external inputs to the system. In fact, the annual recirculation of essential elements such as N, Ca, P, and K, from detritus alone is sufficient to exceed the growth requirements of a northern hardwood forest (Schesinger 1997). Nutrient budgets are the accounting system that balance inputs to the system against outputs over a given time scale. Because they express the cycling process in terms of periodic net gain or loss, nutrient budgets provide one measure of ecosystem health and sustainability.

Soil resources and nutrient cycling are strongly modified by topography and the biota. For example, Johnson and Todd (1990) found that yellow-poplar stands had greater total N, total P, and exchangeable Ca and Mg than oak-hickory and chestnut oak stands, and that total leaching losses were as much as 37% greater from yellow-poplar forests (Johnson et al. 1985). They concluded that slope position and microtopography were more important in determining the rate of nutrient return and overall nutrient status. Boerner (1984) reached a similar conclusion when comparing foliar N and P concentrations of individuals of the same species between southwest-facing and northeast-facing sites. Trees on nutrient-poor, southwest-facing sites were more conservative of nutrients and produced nutrient-poor litter; they had lower maximum foliar N and P concentrations and resorbed a larger proportion of N and P prior to litter fall than did individuals of the same species on mesophytic sites. South- and west-facing slopes are generally warmer, especially in winter (Tajchman 1983); they also have deeper, more heavily weathered and leached soils (Boerner 1984). Where parent materials are similar between sites, north- and east-facing slopes have higher organic matter content, pH, base saturation, and more extractable N than south- and west-facing slopes. In north-central WV, Hicks and Frank (1984) found significant positive correlations between transformed aspect and CEC, organic matter, P, K, Ca, Mg, and total base saturation for soil A, to a lesser extent, B horizons. They attributed this difference, in part, to a more rapid decomposition and recycling rate on north- and east-facing sites. Finally, by avoiding non-preferred plants, deer browsing can favor plants whose leaves may have high lignin concentrations and/or high C:N ratios (Hobbs 1996). Such leaves are mineralized more slowly, causing litter to accumulate.

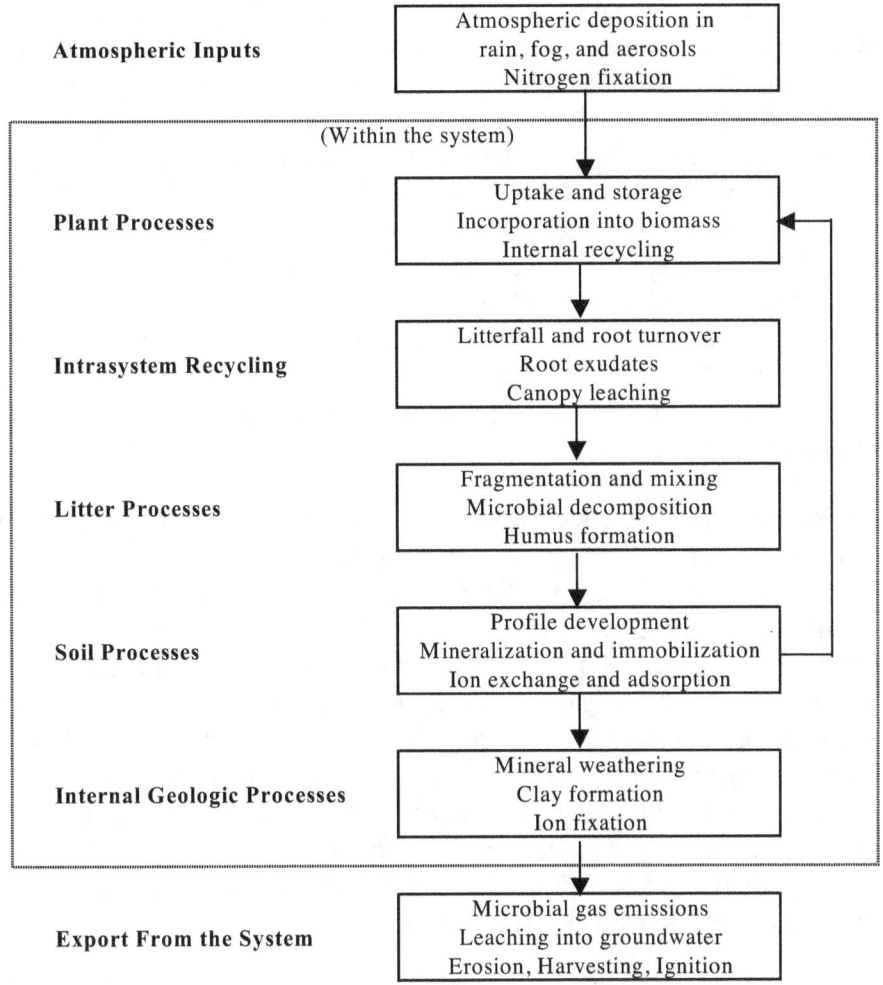

Atmospheric Inputs	Atmospheric deposition in rain, fog, and aerosols Nitrogen fixation

(Within the system)

Plant Processes	Uptake and storage Incorporation into biomass Internal recycling
Intrasystem Recycling	Litterfall and root turnover Root exudates Canopy leaching
Litter Processes	Fragmentation and mixing Microbial decomposition Humus formation
Soil Processes	Profile development Mineralization and immobilization Ion exchange and adsorption
Internal Geologic Processes	Mineral weathering Clay formation Ion fixation
Export From the System	Microbial gas emissions Leaching into groundwater Erosion, Harvesting, Ignition

Figure 7. Conceptual model of processes involved in cycling of minerals through a forest ecosystem (adapted from Waring and Running 1998).

An accurate accounting of inputs and outputs to an ecological system is important for several reasons. First, ecosystem productivity and sustainability is strongly dependent on the total pools of nutrient resources present, their availability, their seasonal fluxes, and whether their long-term status is improving, declining, or remaining static. Productivity also depends on a proper balance of nutrients. Plant tissue is composed of a fairly stable mixture of carbohydrates and macro- and micro-nutrients, and when one nutrient becomes limiting, plants usually do not show deficiency symptoms; they simply grow more slowly (Schlesinger 1997). Input-output budgets are key indicators of variations of soil fertility and the potential sustainability of forest management; they permit managers to anticipate how management activities will initiate soil changes before the impact on soil and vegetation appear (Ranger et al. 1999). Because conservation of forest resources also includes non-timber values such as water quality and control, biodiversity, wildlife habitat, recreational opportunities, and carbon sequestration, for example, nutrient budgets have the potential for far-ranging effects on a wide variety of ecosystem functions and values.

There is strong evidence that human actions can influence nutrient status of a site at macro-, meso-, and micro-scales. For example, at the macro-scale, precipitation in the central Appalachian Region is among the most acidic in the United States, and pH readings below 4.0 are common in summer months (Rentch and Hicks 2000). The buffering of acidic precipitation by forested watersheds is a chemical process that occurs as water from precipitation passes through the ecosystem, and there is an emerging consensus that acid precipitation accelerates nutrient leaching from forest foliage and the soil profile (Helvey and Kunkle 1986; Aber et al. 1998). When combined with the micro-scale activity of timber harvesting on short rotations (i.e., 50–60 yr.), persistently negative budgets may conceivably result in depletion of some essential nutrients and require remedial efforts to restore site productivity (Federer et al. 1989; Long et al. 1997; Adams 1999). Finally, erosional losses and compaction of soils due to visitor use are particularly important for public facilities such as parks.

Functional Groups of Organisms

Chapin et al. (1996) defined functional groups of organisms as groups of species that have similar effects on ecosystem processes. Functional groups are interactive controls because of their capacity to shape the structure and functioning of ecosystems. In this section, we review key functional groups, including vegetation, soil biota, and herbivores.

Vegetation is generally recognized as the dominant functional group in terrestrial ecosystems, and a vast literature has developed over the past 30 years to model ecosystem development and change with regard to vegetation development. These include growth and yield models used in commercial forestry to predict yield (e.g., Clutter 1963; Dale 1972), and models such as OAKSIM, SILVAH, and NE-TWIG. Broader process models have been developed to simulate the temporal and spatial distribution of resources resulting from disturbance and its effects on forest growth, mortality, and recruitment over long periods of time. These include JABOWA (Botkin et al. 1972), SORTIE (Pacala et al. 1993), and FOREST-BGC (Waring and Running 1998).

In additional to conducting photosynthesis, the above-ground structure of vascular plants provides habitat for other organisms and functional groups. Plant litter provides inputs to soil organic matter for recycling. Vegetation structure creates moisture, temperature, and light gradients that are important for biotic diversity. Roots stabilize soils and provide organic matter for below-ground food webs. Vegetation also provides fuel for fire, as well as resources and habitat for below-ground and above-ground consumers and decomposers, ranging from fungi, bacteria, and soil invertebrates to birds and mammals. Carbon storage and mediation of earth-atmosphere energy/water balances are additional ecosystem functions performed by vegetation that are critical for global change processes (Waring and Running 1998; Breshears and Allen 2002). Finally, vegetation provides resources for multiple human values and uses, including consumption of forest products, recreation, and other non-consumptive values.

A large number of vegetation attributes affects the functioning of vegetation in ecosystems. Size, basal area, stem density, biomass, photosynthetic rate, relative and absolute growth rates, tissue chemistry, canopy cover, canopy structure, spatial arrangement, leaf area, and plant longevity are some of the more important and measurable vegetation attributes for ecosystem functioning (Chapin 1993). Reproductive traits, phenology, and shade and moisture tolerance are additional attributes that are particularly important. With respect to disturbance, important functional attributes include palatability, fire tolerance, and modes of post disturbance regeneration.

There have been several regional vegetation classifications for the area encompassing ERMN based on woody canopy cover. Braun (1950) used a physiognomic approach to classify eastern deciduous forest associations. She placed much of the Appalachian Plateau Physiographic Province in the Mixed Mesophytic Forest Region (Figure 8). Notable about this association is the large number of tree species (as many as 25) and species-combinations that may dominate at any particular location (see Figure 9). These include oaks (chestnut, northern red, and white), American beech, yellow-poplar, hemlock, and sugar maple. These associations find their best development on moist, well-drained soils. Braun considered sweet buckeye (*Aesculus flava* Ait.) and white basswood (*Tilia americana* L.) as diagnostic of this forest type. Although it is the overstory layer that primarily characterizes this forest, the understory and herbaceous strata are also diverse, particularly spring ephemerals. East of the Allegheny Front section of the Appalachian Plateau Physiographic Province, the Oak-Chestnut Forest Region is characteristic of the Ridge and Valley and Blue Ridge Physiographic Provinces. Here, oaks (and formerly American chestnut) are so abundant as to characterize the region. The virtual elimination of chestnut by the chestnut fungus (*Cryphonectria parasitica*) beginning in the early 1900s has resulted in increases of several oak and hickory species on drier sites, and by yellow-poplar on more mesic sites (Stephenson et al. 1993). Although it is difficult to draw a sharp boundary between the two forest associations, mesophytic communities are generally confined to moist coves and lower ravine slopes.

Küchler (1964) mapped the United States using potential natural vegetation (PNV), and placed ERMN units in either Mixed Mesophytic or Appalachian oak types. Küchler defined PNV as "the vegetation structure that would become established if all successional sequences were completed without interference by man under the present climatic and edaphic conditions (including those created by man)." Thus the vegetation units are hypothetical units that are thought to indicate a site's potential for developing certain kinds of vegetation. These units are based on known current relationships between vegetation and site characteristics, such as soils or

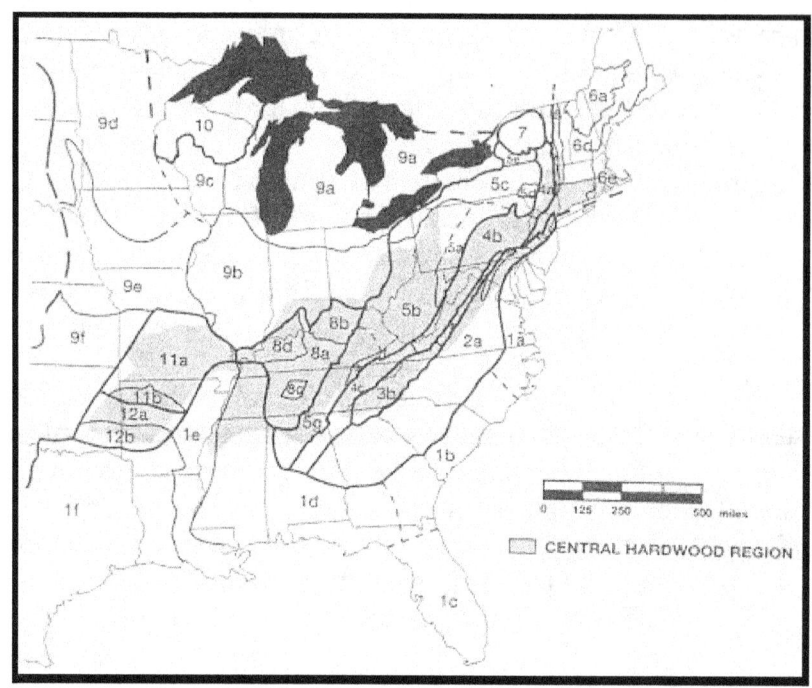

Figure 8. Braun's (1950) vegetational regions and overlay of the central hardwood forest (after Hicks 1998). Region 5 is the Mixed Mesophytic Forest Region, including 5a (Allegheny Mountains), and 5b (Cumberland and Allegheny Plateaus). Region 4 is the Oak-Chestnut Forest Region, including 4a (glaciated section).

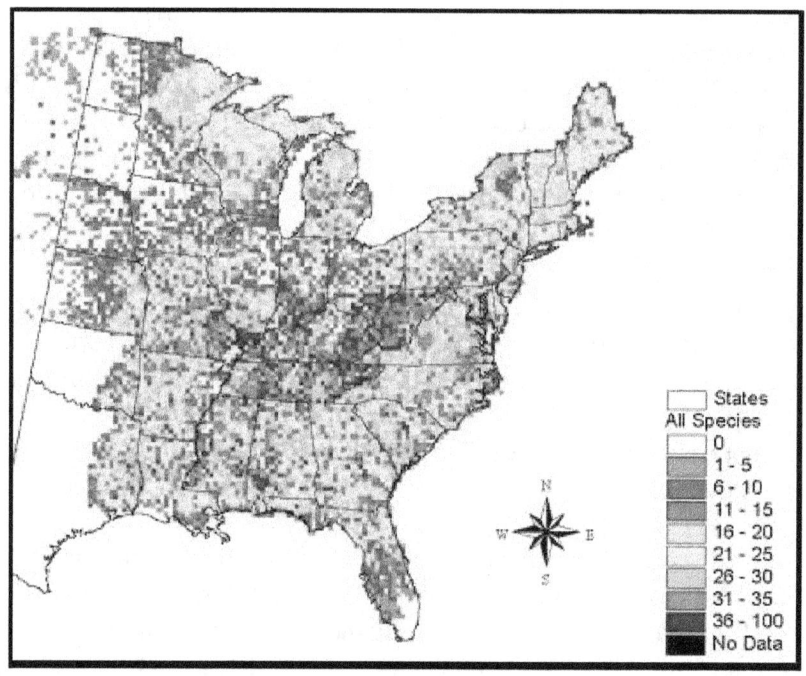

Figure 9. Estimated number of tree species per 20 x 20 km cell, from USDA FS FIA data, and Prasad and Iverson (1999).

landform. They can be used to great advantage by land managers faced with a landscape where much of the vegetation has been removed. However, PNV units are limited by the current knowledge of vegetation-site relationships, and the ability of vegetation per se to infer site characteristics. They also emphasize hypothesized climax vegetation, a concept fraught with theoretical difficulties (e.g., see Gleason 1917, 1926).

Bailey's ecoregion approach (1995) characterized the area encompassing ERMN as either Central Appalachian Broadleaf Forest-Coniferous Forest-Meadow Province (M221) and the Eastern Broadleaf (Oceanic) Province (221) (See Figure 10). The Eastern Broadleaf Forest (Oceanic) Province is characterized by a winter or temperate deciduous forest dominated by tall broadleaf trees that provide a dense, continuous canopy in summer and shed their leaves completely in winter. Lower layers of small trees and shrubs develop weakly. In spring, a luxuriant ground cover of herbs quickly develops, but is greatly reduced after trees reach full foliage and shade the ground. Forest vegetation is divided into three major associations: mixed mesophytic, Appalachian oak, and pine-oak.

In the Central Appalachian Broadleaf Forest-Coniferous Forest-Meadow Province, vertical zonation prevails, with the lower limits of each forest belt rising in elevation toward the south. The Appalachian oak forest is dominated by a dozen species, each in the white oak and black oak groups. Chestnut was once abundant, but now eliminated as a canopy tree. Above this zone lies the northeastern hardwood forest, composed of birch, beech, maple, elm, red oak, and basswood, with an admixture of hemlock and white pine. Mixed mesophytic forest extends into narrow valleys (coves) of the southern Appalachians, where oak vegetation predominates.

Finally, The Nature Conservancy has developed an ecological system matrix for North America (Comer et al. 2003). Their emphasis is on energy flow and nutrient cycling: how processes on the landscape shape ecological systems and define them through a combination of biotic and abiotic criteria. In contrast to Bailey (1995), their classification does not rely on a fixed landscape map unit approach. They define ecological system as a group of plant community types that tend to co-occur within landscapes with similar ecological process, substrates, and/or environmental gradients. These usually manifest themselves at spatial scales of 10s to 1,000s of ha and persist for 50 years or more. Their classification system places all of the units of the ERMN within the Central and Interior Appalachian Division. Omitting exclusively wetland systems, they have identified 32 distinct terrestrial ecological systems (Table 3), 202 associations[1], and 150 systems, as well as acidic, circumneutral, and calcareous barrens.

There have been a number of finer-scale classifications of regional vegetation and vegetation of specific park units. These include gray and peer-reviewed literature that address biotic community composition and ecosystem dynamics within specific park boundaries (e.g., Myers and Irish 1981 [DEWA], Grafton 1982 [NERI], Abrams and Downs 1990 [FRHI], Norris 1992 [BLUE], Grafton 1993 [GARI, BLUE], Evans 1995 [DEWA], Fortney et al. 1995 [GARI, NERI, BLUE], Suiter 1995 [NERI], Sullivan et al. 1998 [DEWA], Young et al. 2001 [DEWA], Mahan et al. 2004 [NERI], Ross et al. 2002 [DEWA], and Rentch et al. 2005 [BLUE]).

---

[1] defined as "a plant community of definite floristic composition, uniform habitat conditions, and uniform physiognomy"
[2] defined as "a physiognomically uniform group of plant associations sharing one or more dominant or diagnostic species."

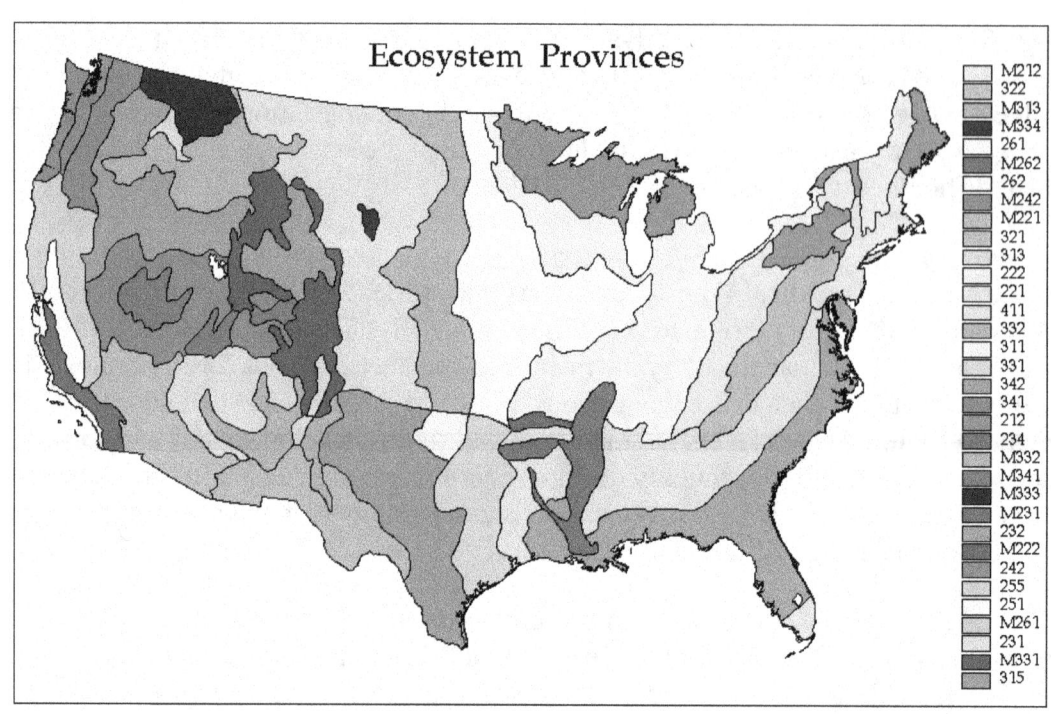

Figure 10. Ecoregions of the United States from Bailey (1995). Province 221 (lime) = Eastern Broadleaf Forest (Oceanic) Province, and M221 (darker green) = Central Appalachian Broadleaf Forest—Coniferous Forest—Meadow Province (available from http://www.fs.fed.us/colorimagemap/ecoreg1_provinces.html).

Table 3. List of upland and mixed upland/wetland ecological systems within the Central and Interior Appalachian Division as identified by The Nature Conservancy present in West Virginia and Pennsylvania (available from: http://www.natureserve.org/getData/ecologyData.jsp.

Forest and Woodland
Allegheny-Cumberland Dry Oak Forest and Woodland
Allegheny-Cumberland Sandstone Box Canyon and Rockhouse
Appalachian (Hemlock)-Northern Hardwood Forest
Appalachian Serpentine Woodland
Appalachian Shale Barrens
Central Appalachian Dry Oak-Pine Forest
Central Appalachian Pine-Oak Rocky Woodland
Central and Southern Appalachian Montane Oak Forest
Central and Southern Appalachian Spruce-Fir Forest
Laurentian-Acadian Pine-Hemlock-Hardwood Forest
North-Central Appalachian Pine Barrens
North-Central Interior Beech-Maple Forest
Northeastern Interior Dry-Mesic Oak Forest
Northern Appalachian-Acadian Rocky Heath Outcrop
South-Central Interior Mesophytic Forest
Southern Appalachian Montane Pine Forest and Woodland
Southern Appalachian Northern Hardwood Forest
Southern and Central Appalachian Cove Forest
Central Appalachian Alkaline Glade and Woodland
Southern Piedmont Glade and Barrens
Steppe-Savanna
Southern and Central Appalachian Mafic Glade and Barrens
Herbaceous
Southern Appalachian Grass and ShrubBald
Mixed Upland and Wetland
Central Appalachian Floodplain
Central Appalachian Riparian
Great Lakes Dune and Swale
South-Central Interior Large Floodplain
South-Central Interior Small Stream and Riparian
Barren
Central Interior Calcareous Cliff and Talus
North-Central Appalachian Acidic Cliff and Talus
North-Central Appalachian Circumneutral Cliff and Talus
Southern Appalachian Montane Cliff and Talus
Southern Appalachian Spray Cliff

Soil biota is a large functional group that is poorly understood but is critical for many of the ecosystem processes described so far (decomposition, mineralization, nutrient cycling, and forest development). Soil biota include microfloral components (bacteria, fungi, and algae), microfaunal components (nematodes, microarthropods, and protozoans), and macrofaunal components (earthworms, ants, and termites). Soil biota also include another significant group, mycorrhizal fungi (MR). These organisms form symbiotic relationships with roots of many plants, a partnership that provides water and nutritional benefits to the host plant in exchange for carbohydrates to the fungi (see Read 1997; Fitter et al. 1999). Recent research has suggested that MR may serve as a carbon conduit, mediating the sharing of carbon sharing between different individuals and/or species (Simard et al. 1997a, 1997b). Another symbiotic relationship involves the N-fixing bacteria and plants. Several common pioneer plant species have N-fixing capabilities due to bacterial associations, including legumes such as black locust (Fabaceae) and alder (Betulaceae).

Herbivores are a broad functional group and they have direct and indirect effects on ecosystem properties and processes. A significant impact of herbivory is its effect on plant species diversity (Gough and Grace 1998). On average, at least 10% of net above-ground primary productivity (NAPP) of terrestrial ecosystems is consumed by grazing herbivores, and it is unlikely that any plant is completely immune from the effects of herbivory. Virtually all plants have traits that reduce the intensity of herbivory to some degree (e.g., lignification, silification, secondary compounds, reduced palatability). Similarly, herbivores display a wide range of feeding morphologies and behaviors that have evolved in response to selection pressures occurring as a result of the evolution of forage plant defenses. Native herbivores include terrestrial invertebrates (grasshoppers, spiders, beetles, moths, etc.), breeding birds (resident or neotropical migrant avifaunal species), small mammals (mice, voles, shrews, chipmunks, and squirrels) and large mammals (white-tailed deer and black bear).

Whether measured by species, individuals, or biomass, invertebrates dominate terrestrial ecosystems (Wilson 1987; Kremen et al. 1993). They occupy the widest possible diversity of ecosystems, microhabitats, and niches, and affect ecosystem processes such as nutrient and water cycling, the regeneration of plant species by pollen and seed dispersal, and the decomposition of dead organic matter (Barnes et al. 1998). In many cases, they directly regulate forest health, growth, and mortality through herbivory (Mattson and Addy 1975). For example, since its introduction in 1869, gypsy moth has become established in 16 states and defoliates millions of acres of hardwood forests annually (Liebhold et al. 1995). Because insect defoliators tend to specialize in one species or genus of species, they can strongly influence the rate and direction of succession (Franklin et al. 1987).

Of all plant-animal mutualisms, insects are probably the most highly co-evolved with plants, particularly with regard to pollination (Baker et al. 1983). In North America, 40 plant families and 69 genera are dominantly or wholly insect pollinated (Haack 1994), including all species of Ericaceae, Fabaceae, and Roseaceae, as well as major forest tree species in the genera *Acer, Aesculus, Lirodendron, Nyssa,* and *Tila*. Despite growing awareness of their importance to conservation monitoring and planning, relatively little attention has been devoted to their inventory and monitoring (Kremen et al. 1993). Both beneficial and detrimental, their invertebrate contributions are critical to forest diversity, soil fertility, and long-term forest health and sustainability (Haack and Byler 1993).

Breeding birds have shown to be useful indicators of ecosystem health, particularly when ecosystems are heavily impacted (Bradford et al. 1998; O'Connell et al. 2000). Many species' distributions are affected by habitat fragmentation (Askins and Philbrick 1987; Wilson et al. 1995), and many birds occupy high trophic levels and may integrate functional disturbance at lower levels (Pettersson et al. 1995; Rodewald and James 1996). They are especially sensitive to habitat features such as canopy structure, nesting sites, food supplies and escape cover (Conner and Dickson 1997), metrics closely associated with vegetative cover and land use. Some species of birds, such as woodpeckers, may serve as indicators of overall bird diversity (Mikusinski et al. 2001). Birds have been shown to be useful indicators of ecosystem health, and this is especially true where ecosystems are heavily impacted (Landres et al. 1988; Bradford et al. 1998; O'Connell et al. 2001). Advantages of long-term monitoring of breeding birds is that historical data already exist regarding populations and distribution (e.g., Yahner et al. 2001, 2004), and there is a sizeable pool of skilled, non-professional observers.

At certain levels, diversity of herbivores contributes to overall diversity and plant community development (see Gough and Grace 1998). However, due to strong interactions of vegetation with nutrient cycling, hydrologic processes, disturbance regimes, and geomorphic processes, herbivore-driven changes in vegetation structure can have cascading effects on many ecosystem processes and properties. For example, chronically high densities of white-tailed deer has led to habitat simplification, compositional and structural changes, and loss of biodiversity (DeCalesta 1994; McShea et al. 2000; Horsley et al. 2003; Rooney and Waller 2003). In some areas deer are now so numerous and destructive as to be identified as a "keystone herbivore" by Waller and Anderson (1997), owing to the profound impact they have on forest ecosystems, including limiting regeneration of woody and herbaceous species.

General Model—Adding Anthropogenic Stressors

Natural ecosystems are complex networks of interacting positive and negative feedbacks (DeAngelis and Post 1991; Chapin et al. 1996; Schlesinger 1997) that operate over a range of temporal and spatial scales. Both feedbacks are important in determining the characteristics of natural ecosystems. Positive feedbacks amplify an initial change and push the ecosystem toward some new state (Chapin et al. 1996). For example, mutualisms of plants with mycorrhizal or N-fixing symbionts create a positive feedback that maximizes productivity because both the host plant and the microbe benefit from the association. In degraded landscapes, mutualisms like this can enhance the resource supply and productivity of the system, demonstrating that positive feedbacks can be ecologically beneficial (Perry et al. 1989). Hydraulic lift by deeply rooted plants distributes deep soil water to surface soil layers to delay daytime water deficit. This benefits both the pumper and neighboring plants that have access to soil moisture (Dawson 1993; Ryel et al. 2002). Population growth also acts as a positive feedback, because increased population size tends to cause still greater population increase. In simple two-species microcosms population growth creates instability, because one species provided with a finite food supply increases its population until the food supply is exhausted, and then the population crashes (Chapin et al. 1996).

In sustainable ecosystems, negative feedbacks constrain positive feedbacks. Negative feedbacks provide resistance and resilience to natural or anthropogenic changes in interactive controls and maintain the potential for recovery and regeneration after disturbance. The acquisition of water, nutrients, and light to support growth of one plant reduces availability of these resources to other plants (Tilman 1988; Oliver and Larsen 1996), thereby, stabilizing community productivity (Chapin and Shaver 1985). Similarly, animal populations cannot sustain exponential population growth indefinitely, because declining food supply and predation (Hairston et al. 1960; Oksanen 1990) reduce the rate of population increase. If these negative feedbacks are weak or absent (e.g., low predation rate), population cycles can amplify and lead to extinction of one or both of the interacting species (Holling 1992).

Both types of feedback are critical for ecosystem development. However, because negative feedbacks are regulatory, they are key to ecosystem sustainability (Chapin et al. 1996). When negative feedbacks are weakened, management must be intensified.

In the following section we outline key terrestrial ecosystem stressors, which we defined earlier as (primarily anthropogenic) disturbances that are either foreign to an ecosystem, or that fall outside the historical range of natural variability. Figure 11 adds impacts of known or hypothesized stressors on interactive controls of the Jenny-Chapin model (Figure 4). In Figure 12 we present a more detailed assessment of relationships between stressors, interactive controls, and primary terrestrial ecosystem processes.

Changes in Landscape Pattern and Process: Habitat Loss and Fragmentation

Fragmentation of the landscape produces a series of patches surrounded by a matrix of different vegetation types and/or land use. Fragmentation may affect key ecosystem attributes such as genetic and species diversity, species density and abundance, interspecific interactions, edge effects, and patch connectivity, and there is a large body of observational and theoretical literature on species, population and community effects of fragmentation (see review, Debinski and Holt 2000, McGarigal and Cushman 2002). Potential harmful effects of fragmentation include initial exclusion, isolation, species-area effects, edge effects, and disruption of natural disturbance regimes (Caley et al. 2001). Many of the species/population responses to fragmentation are driven by changes in the physical environment (Saunders et al. 1991), including alteration of the microclimate (radiation, wind, water flux, etc.) within each remnant patch, and the isolation (a function of patch size, shape, distance between patches, time since isolation, connectivity, etc.) of each from other patches in the surrounding landscape. Monitoring and/or management of these remnants, whether as parks, natural areas, or habitat reserves poses several problems centered on questions of size, shape, and design. The SLOSS (Single Large or Several Small) debate has yet to be resolved (see Simberloff 1988).

The relationship between species diversity and fragmentation is based on the theory of island biogeography (MacArthur and Wilson 1967): species richness in habitat fragments is expected to be a function of island size and isolation. Smaller, more isolated fragments are expected to retain fewer species than larger, less isolated habitat tracts. Genetically, fragmentation reduces genetic variation through genetic drift and inbreeding depression in smaller populations (Templeton et al. 1990). This theory has been verified in many observational studies. For example, Laurance and Bierregaard (1996) found that even in a 100 ha tropical forest, the beetle community was much different in composition and lower in species richness that those on control sites in a continuous forest. Collinge and Foreman (1998) found that insect species diversity was lowest in smallest fragments and highest in largest fragments. In addition, fragmented landscapes also

28

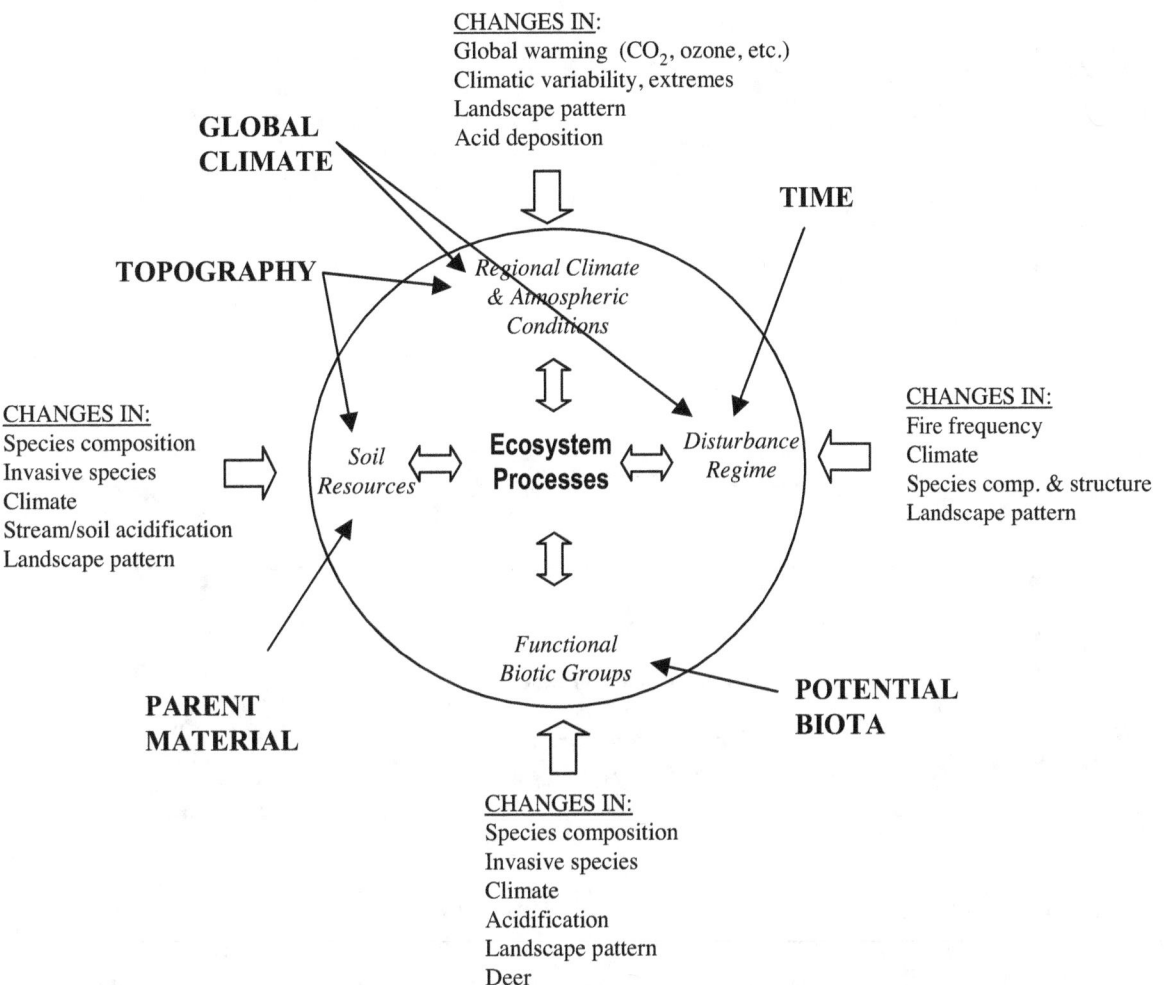

Figure 11 Modified Chapin et al. (1996) ecosystem model of relationship between state factors, interactive controls, and ecosystem processes. State factors are capitalized; interactive controls are italicized, and the circle represents the boundary of the ecosystem. Links between known/hypothesized ecosystem changes and interactive controls are also shown.

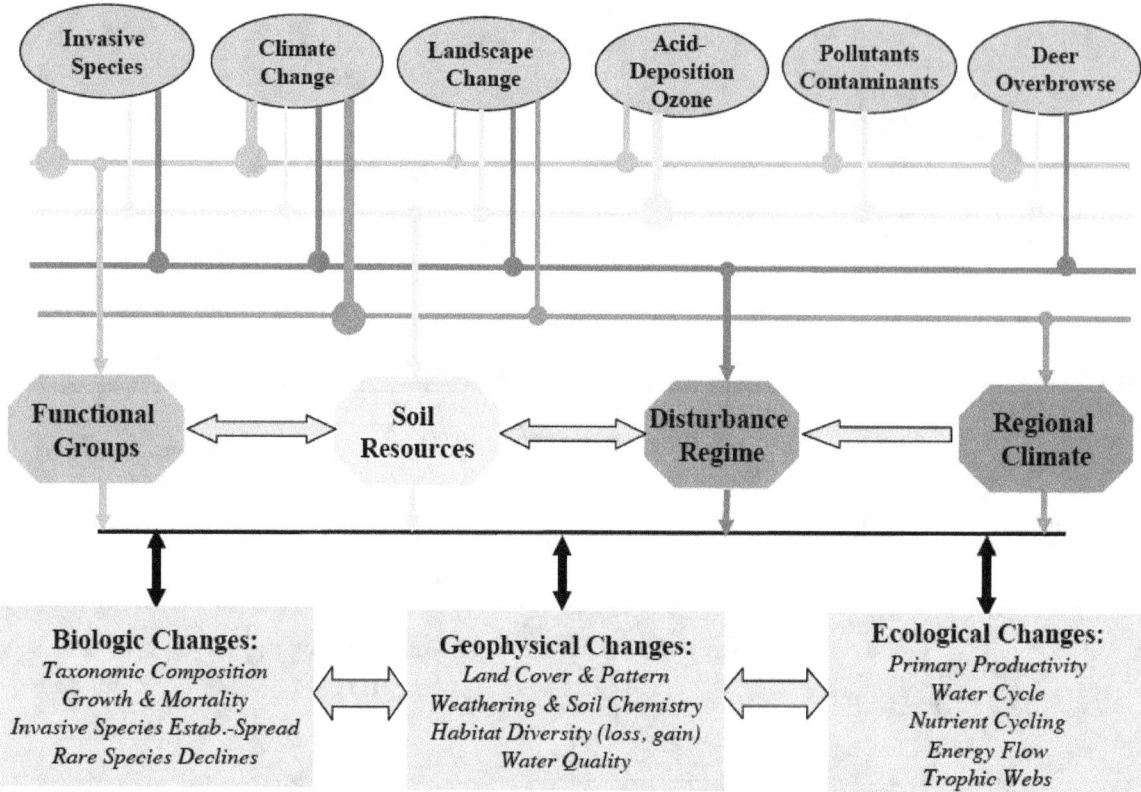

Figure 12. Connections (probable or hypothesized causal linkages) between anthropogenic stressors (ovals), ecosystem interactive controls (octagons), and primary terrestrial ecosystem processes (triangles). Relative impacts of stressors on interactive controls are represented by width of connecting lines.

tend to have lower species abundance and density (Holt et al. 1995; Yao et al. 1999), factors which influence secondary succession and forest development following disturbance.

Spatial dynamics can have profound effects on individual behavior and interspecific interactions such as predation, and fragmentation can mediate or exacerbate shifts in such interactions (Kareiva 1987). Fragmentation creates barriers to dispersal, and behavioral responses to fragmentation, and patch/corridor size/distance may underlie some observed effects at higher organization levels, such as populations and communities. Even narrow breaks (<100 m) in continuous forest habitat may produce substantial barriers to movement of many species of birds and insects (Haddad 1999). Diffendorfer et al. (1995) and Wolff et al. (1997) found that fragmentation reduced movement and altered spatial patterning of several small mammals.

Similarly, edge effects may make habitats more vulnerable to invasion of exotic species and subject it to more extreme biotic influences such as wind and temperature (Saunders et al. 1991). Species that are especially vulnerable to fragmentation include 1) naturally rare species, 2) wide-ranging species, 3) nonvagile species, 4) species with low fecundity, 5) species dependent on patchy, unpredictable resources, 6) species with highly variable population sizes, 7) ground nesters, 8) interior species, and 9) species vulnerable to human exploitation (from online review, available at: http://www.forestry.auburn.edu/mitchell/spatecol/Lectures/fragmentation.pps).

While there is much evidence of the deleterious effects of fragmentation on population and ecosystem dynamics, the multicausal nature of the organism response to fragmentation, complexities of temporal and spatial scaling, time lags, social interactions between species, and the presence habitat generalist species often produce mixed results. For example, reviews of manipulative fragmentation experiments (Debinski and Holt 2000) or observational studies (McGarigal and Cushman 2002) both fail to uniformly verify commonly held hypotheses about the relationship between fragmentation, species richness, density, and other population parameters. Bissonnette and Storch (2002) sum up: the effects of fragmentation are complex and multicausal; exhibit thresholds where they are unexpected; are characterized by time lags that may be unpredictable; are heavily influenced by the structural differences between the matrix and the patches, especially if the patches are disturbance rather than remnant patches; and are heavily dependent on the temporal and spatial scales of the observation. Finally, Bissonnette and Storch (2002) note that dynamics are often contingent on system history and are subject to stochastic events.

Much of the study of effects of habitat loss and fragmentation has been targeted to functional groups, but these changes can potentially affect all four interactive controls. They can result from a wide range of temporal and permanent anthropogenic causes, but all involve the loss and isolation of natural habitats (Meffe et al. 1997). Most studies that involve the effects of habitat fragmentation and edge on avian abundance and diversity also examine the secondary effects of increased predation and cowbird parasitism (Dessecker and Richard 1984, 1987; Yahner and Ross 1995; Yahner and Mahan 1997; Fleming and Giuliano 2001). Although there may be some short-term effects of forestry practices on stream or riparian quality, there is likely not the long-term effects as found with other land uses (Thorton et al. 2000). There is a relatively greater amount of information on the threats of temporary fragmentation and the effects of the resulting edges created to both avian and mammalian species (e.g. Dessecker and Richard 1987; Hoover et al. 1995; Mahan and Yahner 1996; Mahan and Yahner 1999), but only limited information on

31

other taxa. Fredericksen (1998) noted that due to their proximity to ever-enlarging suburban developments, central Appalachian forests are probably more threatened by development than by timber harvesting.

For invertebrate populations, fragmentation and habitat loss may be critical issues, because populations may become increasingly isolated (Saunders et al. 1991). There is little information on how fragmentation may affect genetic variation. From a management perspective, Yahner (1995, 1996, 1997, 1998) details how butterflies and skippers used both native and exotic plants in unmowed and non-pesticide borders of forested and agricultural landscapes.

Recent declines in migratory bird populations breeding in the eastern United States have become a major focus of studies addressing avian conservation and diversity (Robbins et al. 1989; Askins et al. 1990; Yahner and Ross 1995; Yahner and Mahan 1997; Fleming and Giuliano 2001). Fragmentation, degradation, and alteration of breeding grounds, deforestation of tropical winter grounds, and increased nest predation and brood parasitism, coupled with increased edge, are factors that have been associated with observed reductions for many songbird species, including species dependent on grassland and early successional habitats. There have been some studies on the effects of habitat fragmentation as it relates to forestry practices on smaller mammals. The extent to which forestry practices can create different size clearcuts, shapes, proximities, etc., can make assessing (and interpreting) the effects of this type of fragmentation difficult. However, there are some indications that smaller clearcuts may benefit some small mammals, such as the white-footed mouse, by creating areas of low, moist vegetation, although there are other factors, such as food abundance and weather, that may influence how and when small mammals may use forest openings (Yahner 2001).

Changes in Landscape Pattern and Process: Urbanization and Suburbanization

Because expanding human populations require additional space for homes, schools, businesses, etc., some growth is inevitable. However, unmanaged growth characterizes urban sprawl and presents increased negative costs to humans and biodiversity. Typically, urban/suburban sprawl has the following characteristics: 1) low density, 2) unlimited and non-contiguous outward expansion, 3) spatial segregation of different land uses, 4) consumption of and increased pressure on adjoining agricultural lands and environmentally sensitive lands, 5) travel dominance by motor vehicle, 6) small developers operating independently of each other, and 7) lack of integrated land use planning. The effects of urbanization and suburbanization (resulting in land use changes) are felt at all four interactive controls (see Figure 12).

Urban sprawl has been identified as a serious threat to forests and other natural areas, and public concern over impacts has grown in recent years (Bengston et al. 2005). The Southern Forest Resource Assessment (Weir and Greis 2002) found that urbanization has the most direct, immediate, and permanent effects on the extent, condition, and health of southern forests. Although the region encompassing ERMN has not seen some of the same increases in population that other parts of the country have, there have still been problems with sprawl. The five counties surrounding DEWA have experienced some of the most rapid residential development in the United States during the past several decades (250 percent growth during the period 1970 to 1990). Pike County (PA) has been the fastest growing county in Pennsylvania since 1970. Recent estimates indicate local populations have grown by more than 50 percent since 1990.

Furthermore, these census figures do not include the continuing proliferation of vacation homes in the area, because they are not primary residences. The human population in many area developments is three to six times greater during summer weekends and holidays than during the winter. For example, the year-round resident population of one such development (Hemlock Farms) is about 2,500, but on summer weekends this population swells to over 10,000 (from USGS study plan). Sprawl is particularly critical for UPDE, which has only 30 of a potential 75,000 acres in NPS ownership. At NERI, there have recently been several large suburban housing projects proposed for forest land surrounding the park.

This increasing need for more space has prompted a loss of prime farmland and open space, thereby decreasing the amount of land available to all species. However, there are also less obvious effects, including problems with stormwater runoff due such sources as construction, increased asphalt, and pesticide use, which can adversely affect the quality and quantity of water sources in the area. At least two studies have cited evidence that, despite efforts to restore or retain riparian buffer zones, or create detention ponds in urban or suburban areas, the increasing amounts of impervious surfaces in these areas will overwhelm the ability of riparian buffers to control non-point sources of pollution (Booth and Jackson 1997; Hession et al. 2000). The amount of impervious surface within urban areas is also the leading cause of impairment to estuaries surveyed by the National Water Quality Assessment (U.S. EPA 2001).

Changes in landscape pattern and process represent positive feedbacks. Removal of natural cover and increased human population produces additional pressure for more housing, commercial development, and roads, causing further fragmentation and/or loss of natural habitats and losses of biodiversity. These stressors may also threaten non-biotic resources, such as historical and recreational resources, as well as local climate and air and water quality.

Climate Change

Global atmospheric changes attributable to anthropogenic emissions of CO_2 and other greenhouse gases (water vapor, NH_3, NO_x, HFCs, PFCs, SF_6) are expected to have significant environmental and human consequences during this century (Houghton et al. 2001). Interactions between terrestrial ecosystems, ecosystem processes, and climate constitute positive feedbacks. Climate affects primary production and decomposition, which in turn, feed directly back into climate and atmospheric systems by modifying water and greenhouse gas fluxes via evapotranspiration, nitrification and denitrification, and methanogenesis (Ojiwa 1999). In addition, changes in rates of ecosystem processes directly influence rates of change in global environment by modifying land surface properties (e.g., albedo) and the radiant balance. Subak (2005) provided a summary of potential impacts for the Mid-Atlantic states.

Researchers have identified some elements of these changes, but many remain at the modeling or simulation level, while still others are more uncertain. Increasing levels of atmospheric CO_2, as well as rising air, water, and soil temperatures and altered precipitation patterns (including changes in the frequency and intensity of extreme events such as droughts, storms, hurricanes, or tornadoes) have the potential to effect species' physiological processes and distributions, competitive relations, and population dynamics of plants, nutrient cycling, hydrological processes, and disturbance regimes. Most affected will be species that are near the edge of their optimum range, or species of concern whose population dynamics are already imperiled.

Several researchers have simulated distributional shifts in plant populations in response to anticipated twofold increase in CO_2 concentrations over the next century, using global climate change models (see Iverson et al. 1999; Hanson et al. 2001; Malcolm et al. 2002). Iverson et al. (1999) reviewed the distribution of 80 tree species in the eastern U.S. and found that 30 species could expand their range by at least 10%, while ranges of an additional 30 could decrease by 10%. As many as four to nine species, including sugar maple, black cherry, and trembling aspen (see Figure 13), would potentially move out of the United States to the north. Nearly half showed the potential to shift their ecological optima 100 km (62 mi)north. Iverson et al. (2004) caution, however, that historic rates of migration (10–50 km/100 yr [6–31 mi/100 yr]) will not likely occur, given the currently fragmented landscape (an unexpected negative feedback). Observed responses to climate change include latitudinal and range shifts of shrubs in Alaska (Sturm 2001), birds in the U.K. (Thomas and Lennon 1999), and red fox in Canada (Hersteinsson and MacDonald 1992). Additional observed responses included altered plant (Bradley et al. 1999) and bird, amphibian, and butterfly (Walther et al. 2002) phenology, accelerated invasions of introduced species (Walther 2000; Dale 2001), changes in nesting behavior of Canada geese (MacInnes et al. 1990), and changes in sex ratios of painted turtles due to summer temperature shifts (Janzen 1994).

Local, regional, and global climate changes can also influence occurrence, timing, frequency, duration, extent, and intensity of disturbances (Turner et al. 1998;, Dale et al. 2001). For example, the frequency, size, intensity, seasonality and type of fire depend on weather and climate, in addition to fuel supply, forest structure, and composition. The Canadian Climate Center Model (CGCM1) predicts a 30% increase in the seasonal severity rating of fire hazard for the southeastern United States, and 10% increases elsewhere, which amounts to a 25–50% increase in total area burned (Dale et al. 2001). Climate also affects survival and spread of insects and pathogens, as well as the susceptibility of forest ecosystems. This could mean increased disturbance in some areas and decreased disturbance in others. For example, an increase in minimum winter temperatures is expected to favor more northerly outbreaks of southern pine beetles, but could reduce southerly outbreaks (Ungerer at al. 1999). Climate may also affect frequency and intensity of windstorms, the most important form of abiotic disturbance in eastern deciduous forests, although simulations of these effects are tentative because these smaller scale events are below the resolution of current climate models. Berz (1993) suggests that increased intensity of all atmospheric processes will accelerate the frequency and intensity of windstorms, and Karl et al. (1995) found that the climate of the U.S. has already become more extreme in recent decades.

Air and Water Pollution

Pollution includes atmospheric pollutants, such as aerosols, particulates, ozone, and cumulative deposition of hydrogen ion (H+), nitrogen (NO_x, NH_3) and sulfur (SO_4) via wet and dry processes, as well as those that enter the ecosystem primarily through the water supply, described as point or non-point pollution. By contamination of soil resources and surface waters, pollution stresses terrestrial and aquatic functional groups, and therefore poses a threat to ecosystem processes.

Figure 13. Estimated range shifts of sugar maple under a 2x CO_2 concentration increase, using the GISS climate model (from Prasad and Iverson 1999).

Air and Water Pollution: Acid Deposition

Acid deposition results from release of sulfur and nitrogen oxides during the burning of fossil fuels, automobile exhaust, and other industries. It can occur as either wet (rain or snow) or dry deposition, as particles or vapor, or as cloud or fog deposition (Driscoll et al. 2001). When these pollutants mix with water vapor, sulfur and nitric acids are formed. Chronic acidification generally refers to streams, lakes, and soil ecosystems that have lost their ability to neutralize acidifying events. Episodic acidification typically occurs during periods of high stream flow associated with rainstorms or snowmelt and is, by definition, a short-term decrease in acid neutralizing capacity. Base nutrients, such as calcium, potassium, and magnesium, and other types of neutralizing chemicals, normally buffer changes in ecosystem acidity. However, when ecosystems are exposed to excessive, long-term acid deposition, these chemicals can become depleted. This can make the system more vulnerable to episodic acidification events and may lead to chronic surface-water acidity, as well as nitrogen saturation of forest soils (see Aber et al. 1998).

In the Adirondack region of New York, a U.S. EPA Ecosystem Monitoring and Assessment Program (EMAP) survey reported that 41% of the 1,812 lakes are either chronically acidic or sensitive to episodic acidification during 1991–1994 (Stevens 1994). Kram et al. (2001) reconstructed historical patterns of deposition at Hubbard Brook Experimental Forest (HBEF) in Hew Hampshire and found soil percentage base saturation declined to about 10% in response to acidic deposition, and that this deposition has also resulted in a 4x increase in stream SO_4, a decrease in acid neutralizing capacity from positive to negative values, a decrease in stream pH, and toxic increases in streamwater aluminum. Since 1964, there have been reductions of SO_4 emissions and deposition at HBEF. In addition, there has been a long-term decrease in stream concentrations of NO_3 (that have not been associated with either declines in emissions or bulk deposition) that has resulted in small, but significant increases in stream pH (Likens et al. 2001).

Similar trends were noted in Pennsylvania by Lynch et al. (2000), from the wet deposition monitoring network started in 1981 (see Figure 14, Schneck et al. 1999, for period 1995–1998). Trends include: 1) a precipitation-weighted mean annual pH of 4.20 in 2000 (15 sites), ranging from 4.20–4.37; 2) in general, precipitation in the western half of the state was more acidic; 3) although pH was slightly more acidic in 2000 than in 1999, precipitation is still less acidic than in the 1980s or early 1990s—statistically significant trends of decreasing acidity are evident at all monitoring sites within the state from 1983–2000; and 4) nitrate concentrations were not as sharply lower as sulfate concentrations. Although nitrogen oxide emissions have declined at utility sources targeted by the Clean Air Act Amendments, other sources of nitrogen oxide emissions have increased from both industrial and mobile sources (Figure 15).

There are many reviews on the effects of acid precipitation on aquatic ecosystems (Lynch and Corbett 1980; Sharpe 1990; Bradt 1994; Driscoll et al. 2001), and there have also been many individual studies on the effects of acid precipitation on forests (Taylor et al. 1994; Driscoll et al. 2001), as well as water quality, and fish and macroinvertebrate populations. There have been a number of studies in the Laurel Hill area of southwestern Pennsylvania, where acidic conditions have been comparatively high during the last two decades (e.g. DeWalle et al. 1982; DeWalle et al. 1987; Sharpe et al. 1987; Kimmel et al. 1996; Sharpe and Demchik 1998). There is also a comparatively large amount of information on the effects of acidity on amphibian

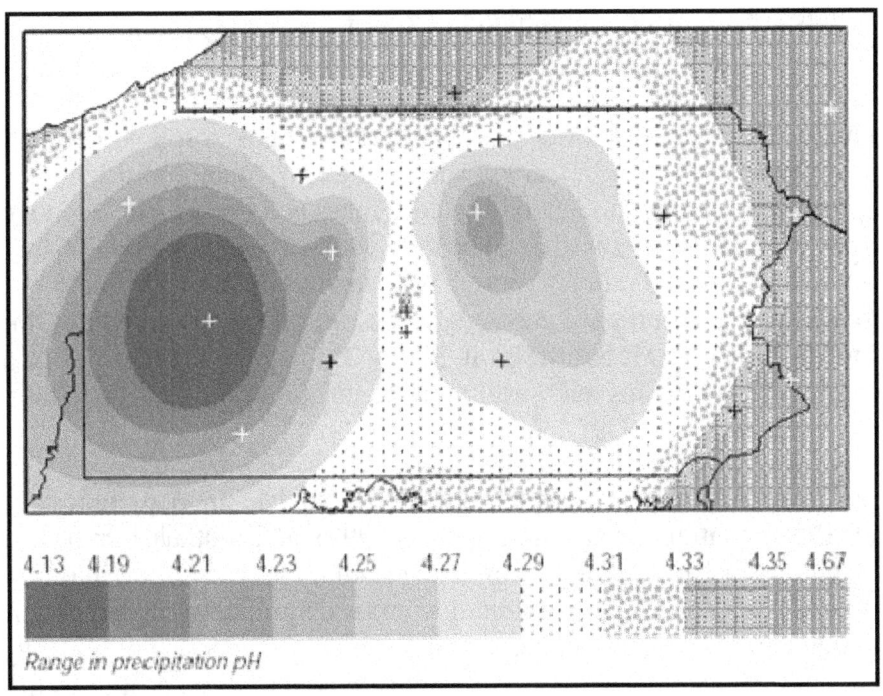

Figure 14. Mean annual pH of precipitation in Pennsylvania, 1995–1998 (cited in Schneck et al. 1999).

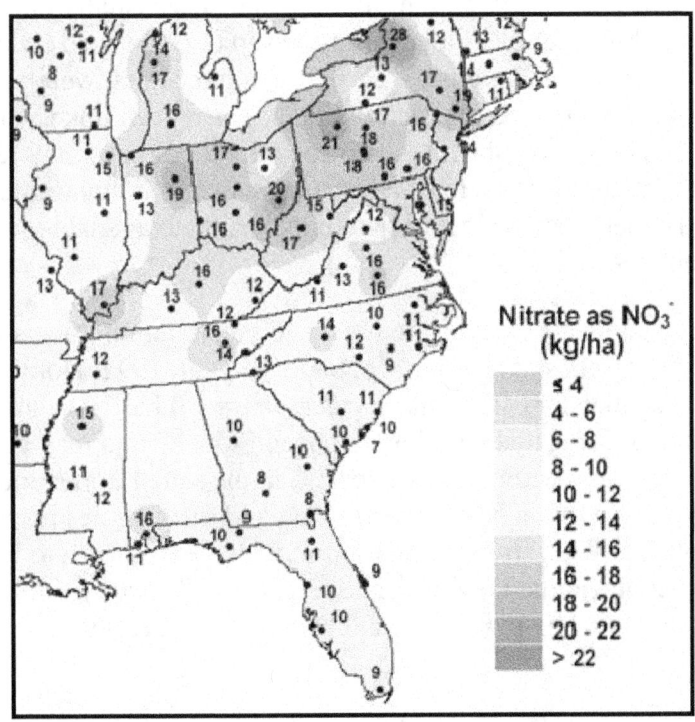

Figure 15. Inorganic nitrogen wet deposition from N-nitrate, 2003 (adapted from http://nadp.sws.uiuc.edu/isopleths/maps2003/no3dep.pdf).

populations as compared to other potential threats (e.g. Freda and Dunson 1985, 1986; Dunson et al. 1992).

Acidic precipitation can cause both short- and long-term changes in soil nutrients, thereby changing the availability of these necessary nutrients to trees. Acid deposition disrupts leaf-level Ca-associated processes, leading to reduction in cold-tolerance (3-10 C) and shoot dieback of red spruce (DeHaynes et al. 1999), and is also associated with soil calcium depletion, aluminum mobilization, and reduced Ca:Al ratios. These have been associated with fine root dysfunction, reducing uptake of water and nutrients, particularly Ca (Shortle and Smith 1988; McLaughlin et al. 1991; Cronan and Grigal 1995; Shortle et al. 1997). Damage to the root tips of trees by increased aluminum concentrations may result in reduced ability for the tree to take up calcium and magnesium (Dehayes et al. 1999; Schneck et al. 1999).

At the ecosystem level, acid precipitation has been linked to calcium depletion in northeastern (Lawrence et al. 1995), central Appalachian (Adams 1999), and southeastern forests (cited in Lawrence and Huntington 1999). Calcium and magnesium may also leach into the water due to an increase in positive ions from acid precipitation and are ultimately carried downstream, thereby unavailable to plants or trees. There is evidence that the decline of both sugar maples and northern red oaks in areas of Pennsylvania may be linked to these processes (see Long et al. 1997; Horsley et al. 1999; Demchek and Sharp 2004).

In Europe, Bobbink et al. (1998) noted that long-term nitrogen enrichment led to competitive exclusion of characteristic species by more nitrophilic plants, especially under oligo- to mesotrophic conditions. For example, Falkengren-Grerup (1995) found species of *Urtica*, *Epilobium*, *Stellaria*, *Galium*, and *Sambucus*, all nitrogen indicators, were more common nitrogen-enriched sites in Europe. Acid precipitation has also been linked to increased susceptibility of trees to pests or pathogens. Predisposition to disease may result from altered resource allocation or carbon metabolism; if additional demands are placed on carbon resources for defense compounds, there may be insufficient photosynthate available for other tree processes (Taylor et al. 1994).

There have been a large number of studies on how acid precipitation affects the reproduction and viability of salamanders in Pennsylvania (Rowe, Sadinski et al. 1992; Horne and Dunson 1994, 1995). The Jefferson Salamander (*Ambystoma jeffersonianum*) has been shown to be sensitive to conditions of low pH (and associated aluminum concentrations), and may be the major factor responsible for the successful breeding of this species in the state (Horne and Dunson 1994, 1995). There is less information on how different frog and toad species respond to acid precipitation , although the Wood frog (*Rana sylvatica*) has been shown to be more tolerant of low pH conditions. In contrast, the Fowler's toad (*Bufo woodhouseii fowleri*) shows significantly slower growth at low pH (Freda and Dunson 1986) and is absent from the most acidic ponds.

Landscape metrics such as land use and site history play a significant role in preconditioning the forest response to nitrogen deposition (Aber et al. 1998; Goodale and Aber 2001). The greater the previous extraction of nitrogen (by agriculture, fires, or forest harvesting), the greater the nitrogen limitation, and the larger the amount of nitrogen deposition necessary to move a site toward saturation. Time periods involved may be as large as 100–200 years. Over all, Aber et al. (1998) found that previous land-use history was as important as either total or current nitrogen deposition in determining current leaching losses in the northeastern U.S.

Air and Water Pollution: Ozone

Ozone has often been cited as the air pollutant of greatest direct threat to vegetation in the eastern U.S. (EPA 1996). At ground level, ozone is a major constituent of photochemical smog that occurs when nitrogen oxides and volatile organic compounds react in the atmosphere in the presence of sunlight. It is primarily an urban pollutant, but can travel long distances, resulting in high concentrations in national parks. Ozone affects human health, causing respiratory problems. In addition, ozone affects vegetation, causing foliar injury and premature aging of leaves, destruction of the photosynthetic enzymes, (i.e., Rubisco), and thereby, leading to a reduction in growth. Chronic ozone exposure has three main physiological effects on plants: 1) disruption of transpiration; 2) disturbances in carbohydrate metabolism and movement; and 3) mineral nutrient deficiencies. All of these lead to premature leaf aging, yellowing, and reductions in growth rates (Chappeklka and Samuelson 1998).

Most research on effects of ozone on growth has concentrated on effects on agricultural crops. Reich and Amundson (1985) reported a net reduction in net photosynthesis in crops for all species tests. Wang et al. (1986) also found that ozone reduced tree growth rates, and that some of the reductions occurred at rates below ambient air quality standards. Chappelka and Samuelson (1998) found that ozone sensitivity is affected by species, tree developmental stage, microclimate, and the ability to compensate for ozone injury through enhanced leaf production and alterations in carbon partitioning. They conclude, however, that clearly defined cause and effect relationships between visible injury and growth losses have not been demonstrated. Thus, for example, Edwards et al. (2004) found patterns of exceedances of 8 hr ambient ozone standards in the central Appalachians between 1988–1999, but they suggested that negative vegetation responses were minimal at most monitoring sites, at least in the short term.

There is also a positive feedback mechanism between ozone and acid deposition. Chronic ozone exposure may lead to mineral nutrient deficiencies, as ions and organic compounds are leached from leaves. Greater uptake of minerals from soil may compensate for leaching; however, soil acidification may reduce the availability of soil nutrients due to leaching and aluminum release. Chappelka and Chevonne (1992) conclude that the literature also indicates that ozone has the potential to influence tree reproduction, directly by affecting reproductive structures, and indirectly by affecting plant metabolism.

Air and Water Pollution: Point- and Non-point Source Pollutants and Contaminants

Non-point source pollution typically originates from a wide variety of sources and typically enters a waterway from either snowmelt or rainwater moving over ground, disrupting the immediate stream or lake area as well as those areas downstream. There are many sources for this type of pollution, including nutrients, such as phosphorus and nitrogen, from agricultural lands, runoff of sediments and chemicals from construction and development projects, herbicides and pesticides from lawns, drilling for oil and gas, and acid precipitation (EPA 1993). Agriculture and abandoned mines currently are the two largest contributors to non-point source pollution in the state (Arway 1999; PADEP 2001). Eutrophication of the Chesapeake Bay has been, in part, attributed to upstream pollution. Acid mine drainage, in particular, has been identified as a significant natural resource issue at several facilities in ERMN (Marshall et al. 2004). Point-source pollution originates from a discrete source and includes sewage treatment plants and industrial plants, where the pollution is typically discharged directly into a waterway. Programs to control the amount of point-source pollution have been more successful than non-point sources pollution programs in reducing pollutants entering waterways.

During the last decade, a significant number of amphibian limb abnormalities have been reported across the country. Although the northern leopard frog (*Rana pipiens*) is the most commonly reported species with deformities, many other species have been reported as well. In Pennsylvania, four counties have reported either frogs or newts with deformities (not all counties have been surveyed). The causes are still not completely understood, although possible sources include an increase in UV-B radiation, increased use of pesticides and other toxins, and an increase in nematode infections brought on by other causes. (See North American Reporting Center for Amphibian Deformities, at http://www.npsc.nbs.gov/narcam/).

There are some studies to suggest that various contaminants may have contributed to the decline of raptor species such as the Cooper's hawk (see review in Pattee et al. 1985). More recently, an examination of contaminants of the possibly declining sharp-shinned hawk revealed that DDE, PCB's, and mercury were detected in high, but sub-lethal levels on the Kittatinny Ridge in eastern Pennsylvania (Wood et al. 1996). It is still unknown if the sub-lethal concentrations of these and other compounds can cause impairment or reproductive losses. There is very little literature on the effects of various threats on any bryophyte species. The Pennsylvania Biological Survey report (Manville and Webster 1998) lists the major threat as air pollution. Engleman and McDiffett (1996) found that bryophytes accumulated more iron in sites that were more acidic due to abandoned mine drainage, and accumulated more aluminum in sites that had more neutral pH. However, the reasons for this are not completely understood. Although lichens can be used as an indicator of air quality (Showman and Long 1992), there are few lichen inventories in the region (Manville and Webster 1998).

Introduced/Invasive Species

Concern over the ecological impacts of invasive organisms is nearly uniform among ERMN units and others in the NPS system. Threats range from benign to severe, although it is usually difficult to predict how an introduced species will behave as it is introduced and becomes established (Slobodkin 2001), particularly given the interacting effects of other stressors such as climate change, acid deposition, forest fragmentation, etc. Invasive plants can directly affect native plants by becoming either monopolizers or donors of limiting resources. They can indirectly affect native communities by altering soil stability, promoting erosion, colonizing open substrates, affecting the accumulation of litter, salt, and other soil resources, and promoting or suppressing fire (Richardson et al. 2000; Brooks et al. 2004). While all of these effects have been identified, it is often difficult to separate out the effects of invasive plants from the effects of other anthropogenic disturbances—in fact, they are intricately linked.

Invasive species capitalize on many techniques in order to invade ecosystems. D'Antonio and Vitousek (1992) identified three ways that biological invasions alter ecosystems: 1) they alter rates of resource supply; 2) trophic level relationships; and 3) the disturbance regime. These relationships are depicted in the context of altering interactive controls in Figure 12. Invasive plants compete with native plants for resources, and competition is most severe for threatened and endangered species. Of the federally threatened and endangered species listed in the United States, 42% are threatened by nonnative species (TNC 1996; Pimentel 1999), and alien species were the second-ranked threat after habitat degradation (Wilcove et al. 1998). Invasives may also out-compete native plants that are food supplies for animals in the ecosystem. This may result in animals depending on nonnative plants for food or, if they are specialists, losing their food source entirely. Invasive species can alter trophic food webs (D'Antonio and Vitousek 1992). An invading species can act as a new predator or a new food source, thereby altering the normal relationships within an ecosystem. Invasive plants usually have no predators in their new environments and they may out-compete an important food source for native animals. In addition, invasives can hybridize with closely related indigenous plants, sometimes creating even more aggressive invaders (Mallet 2005). Contemporary problems with native plants, such as reed canary grass (*Phalaris arundinacea*) and cattail (*Typha* x *glauca*), have been linked to hybridization of native and exotic genotypes (Galatowitsch et al. 1999).

Some invasive plants have been implicated in changing the hydrology and salinity of an area. Salt-cedar (*Tamarix*) species alter the desert riparian areas that they invade in the American southwest through increasing evapotranspiration, adding to the desiccation of flood plains (Walker and Smith 1997). Yellow iris (*Iris acorus*) was instrumental in changing a Potomac River marsh to mesic forest by creating a raised seed bed with its rhizomes that favored ash trees over willows (Woods 1997). Introductions may also alter historical natural disturbance regimes. Spread of the annual, Japanese stilt grass (*Microstegium vimineum*), into natural areas after disturbance may result in monospecific understory stands that impede tree regeneration. During the growing season, forest floors dominated by this flammable grass are increasingly prone to fire, while during the dormant season, bare ground is increasingly subject to soil erosion from winter rains (Hunt and Zaremba 1992). The introduction of cheat grass in the intermountain west has been partially responsible for the alteration of the fire frequency on grasslands from a 50-year to a 5-year return interval (D'Antonio and Vitousek 1992; Pimentel et al. 1999). *Malaleuca quinquenervia* has had a similar effect in Florida (Mack et al. 2000).

Introduced insects and diseases pose more direct ecological consequences. Pests and diseases are integral parts of healthy forests. It is only when they reach levels where natural adaptations are not effective in limiting damage that they significantly affect forest processes. Introduced terrestrial fungal and invertebrate species have the potential to greatly impact resources of ERMN by directly altering host species regeneration, growth, and mortality rates, and subsequently, forest vigor, composition, and structure. Large-scale damage, such as defoliation and mortality caused by forest pests, can cause losses of valuable visual and scenic qualities, recreational opportunities, watershed integrity, wood products, and wildlife habitat. Resource losses from some outbreaks have been spectacular. The chestnut blight fungus, *Cryphonectria parasitica*, virtually eliminated American chestnut throughout its range, and resulted in significant changes in forest composition and structure. Beech bark disease (*Nectria coccinea* var *faginata*), Dutch elm disease (*Ophiostoma ulmi*), emerald ash borer (*Agrilus planipennis*), and others promise similar results with respect to their hosts, American beech, American elm, and ash species, respectively. Since 1885, gypsy moth (*Lymantria dispar*) infestations have caused substantial damage because their preferred host tree species, including oaks, play such dominant roles in eastern forests (Liebhold et al. 1995). On the horizon is an even more threatening disease, Sudden Oak Death Syndrome (SOD), caused by a *Phytopthera* fungus that poses severe threats to the oak-dominated forestlands of the region.

Since its introduction in Virginia during the 1950s, the hemlock woolly adelgid (*Adelges tsugae*) has spread north, south, and west, with significant mortality impacts on eastern and Carolina hemlock (see Figure 16). At Shenandoah National Park in Virginia, where the adelgid has been present since 1988, less than 10% of hemlocks sampled still have 90–100% of foliage intact; very few stands are entirely free of the adelgid (Barr 2002). Mortality has also been high in DEWA, where hemlock and mixed stands comprise nearly 20% of the total forest acreage (Mahan et al. 2004). Sixteen percent of sample hemlocks there were dead, and 27% showed moderate to severe decline in 2002 (Evans 2003). According to the NPS (USDI 2000), the decline of hemlock in the Delaware Water Gap National Recreation Area is likely to have "massive adverse effects on the ecological, aesthetic, and recreational values of the park. Affected streams would be warmer, have lower water flows, and are more likely to dry up during summer droughts. Overall species diversity in hemlock-dominated habitats will probably decline by 35% or more. Decaying and downed trees would increase debris flow, interfere with water flow, and cause channel scouring that would raise the chance of extreme flood damage. Nutrient cycling would also be disturbed" (Jenkins et al. 1999). Studying hemlock mortality at DEWA, Eschtruth et al. (no date) also found that there was a potential for significant increase in exotic invasive plants. Control methods include use of insecticides and introduction of biological control agents. Pesticides are impractical on a landscape scale and not recommended in riparian zones. Identification, selection, mass production, and successful establishment of biological control agents in infested stands are still in the developmental stages, although some promising results have been noted (see Cheah et al. 2005).

White-tailed Deer

Considerable controversy has arisen over management of white-tailed deer in eastern deciduous forests. By the early 1900s, commercial and private exploitation had led to near extirpation. By the late 1900s, the clearing of forestland for agriculture and timber, the extirpation of predators, and the formation of state game protective management agencies and regulatory laws combined to increase deer populations, producing estimates that were 2–5 times greater than presettlement era values (see Figure 17) (Horsley et al. 2003; Rooney and Waller 2003). Because of deer's propensity to restructure whole ecological communities, several researchers (e.g., Waller and Alverson 1997; Rooney and Waller 2003) have identified deer as keystone herbivores (although note that Russell et al. [2001] contend that well-supported experimental measures of the magnitude and geographical extent of deer effects have not been proven convincingly.).

Studies of effects of deer browse date to the 1940s. Most early studies fenced out deer (exclosures) and noted recovery of protected habitat (e.g., Marquis 1974, 1981). Although these provided sometimes dramatic pictures of the effects of browse, they suffered at least two limitations. They provided only two points of reference (no deer, ambient deer density) that concealed non-linear relationships between deer density and browse, and plant community condition. They were, in addition, somewhat unrealistic since zero deer densities were unlikely to occur, nor were they desired. More recent studies have fenced in deer at varying densities (enclosure studies), and attempted to correlate ecosystem effects with known deer density, looking in particular, for non-linear relationships (e.g, Horsley et al. 2003).

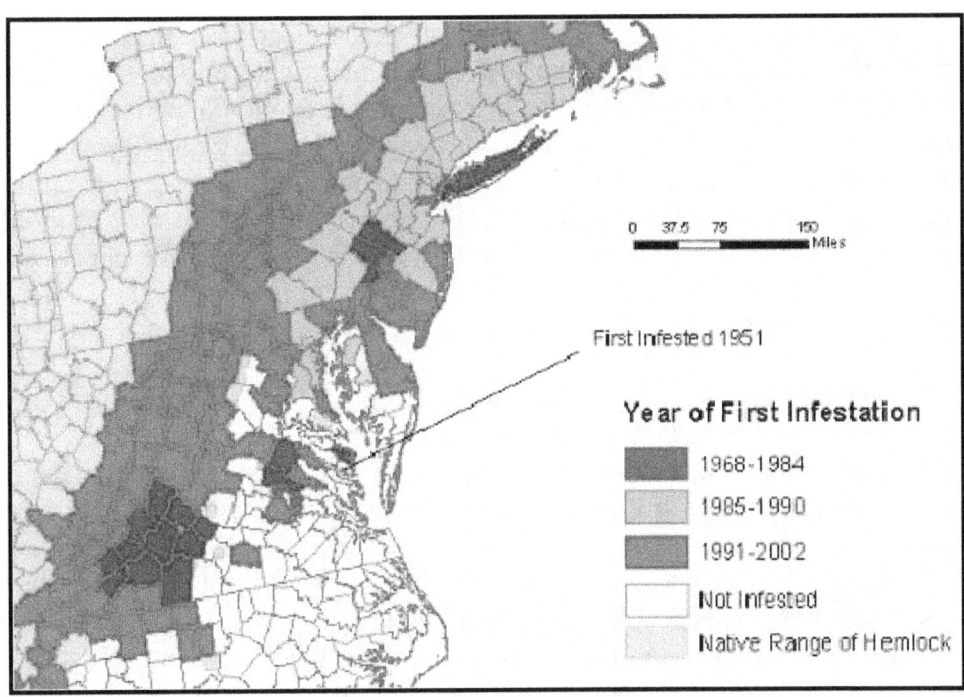

Figure 16. Hemlock woolly adelgid infestations, 1951–2002. Available from USDA Forest Service, http://www.fs.fed.us/na/morgantown/fhp/hwa/maps/hwa_hist2.jpg.

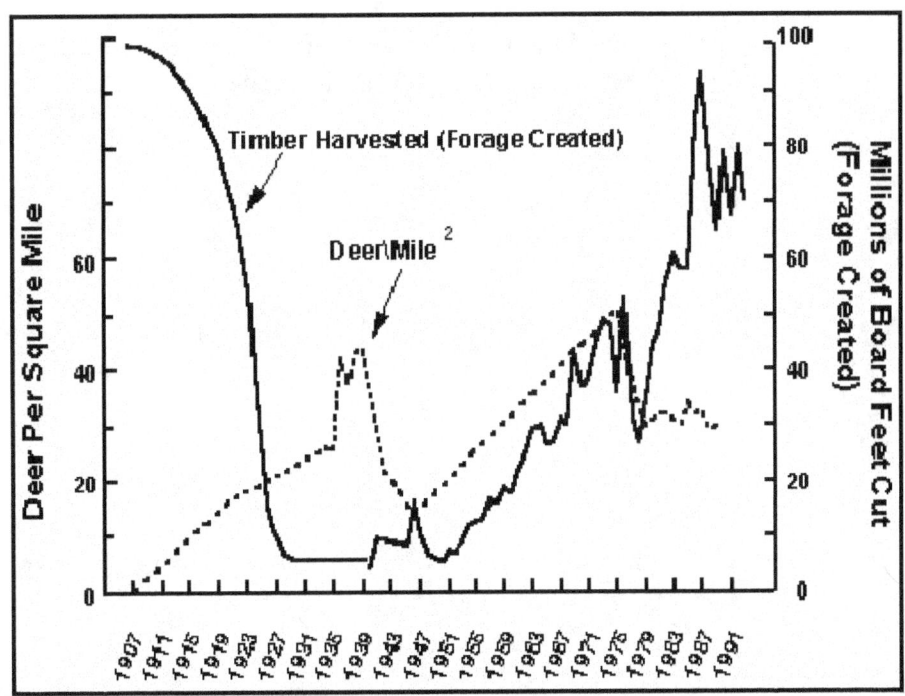

Figure 17. Deer density vs. timber harvesting, 1907–1991, Pennsylvania. From deCalesta (no date).

Direct effects of white-tailed deer include selective browsing that causes changes in species composition, reduction in woody species density and height growth (horizontal structure, Rossell et al. 2005), changes in vertical structure (i.e., browse line), reduction in herbaceous abundance, height, diversity (Frelich and Lorimer 1985; Rooney and Waller 2001; Horsley et al. 2003; McGraw and Furedi 2005), and in terms of forest management, tree regeneration failures (Marquis and Brenneman 1981; Rooney et al. 2002). Some avian species may benefit from structural changes, i.e., decrease in vertical cover, however the loss of cover can also increase avian predation on shrub-nesting birds, and result in declines in overall songbird diversity and abundance (DeCalesta 1994; Flowerdew and Ellwood 2001).

Indirect effects include interference by browse-resistant species with establishment of preferred species, exhaustion of seed bank (e.g. pin cherry and blackberry), and altered food webs as preferred plant species are over browsed and sometimes extirpated by deer. High deer densities have resulted in habitat simplification, where understorys are dominated by monospecific stands of nonpalatable vegetation, such as mountain maple, hay-scented fern, and New York fern (Rooney et al. 2001). Finally, changes in plant community composition due to overbrowsing by deer are linked to altered nutrient cycling. By avoiding non-preferred species, deer browsing can favor plants whose leaves may have high lignin concentrations and/or high C:N ratios (Hobbs 1996). Such leaves are mineralized more slowly, causing litter to accumulate. Alternately, mineralization rates may be increased in forests where the canopy composition has shifted from conifers to hardwoods, in part, due to browsing (Frelich and Lorimer 1985). By modifying litter quality and mineralization rates, deer can thus affect site productivity, creating negative or positive feedbacks affecting the abundance of other understory and canopy species.

To guide the monitoring program and the vital sign selection process, we present a list of proposed vitals signs (prepared by Hicks et al. 2005) in the Appendix.

Literature Cited

Aber, J., R. P. Neilson, S. McNulty, J. M. Lenihan, D. Bachelet, and R. J. Drapek. 2001. Forest processes and global environmental change: predicting the effects of individual and multiple stressors. BioScience 51:735–751.

Aber, J., W. McDowell, K. Nadelhoffer, A. Magill, G. Bernston, M. Kameakea, S. McNulty, W. Currie, L. Rustad, and I Fernandez. 1998. Nitrogen saturation in temperate forest ecosystems. BioScience 48:921–934.

Abrams. M. D. 1992. Fire and the development of oak forests. BioScience 42:346–353.

Abrams, M. D. 1998. The red maple paradox. BioScience 48:355–364.

Abrams, M. D. 2000. Fire and the ecological history of oak forests in the eastern United States. *In* Yaussey, D. A., comp. Proceedings: workshop on fire, people, and the central hardwoods landscape. USDA Forest Service, Gen. Tech. Rep. NE-247.

Abrams, M. D., and J. A. Downs. 1990. Successional replacement of old-growth white oak by mixed mesophytic hardwoods in southwestern Pennsylvania. Can. J. For. Res. 20:1864–1870.

Abrams, M. D., and M. L. Scott. 1989. Disturbance-mediated accelerated succession in two Michigan forest types. For. Sci. 35(1):42–49.

Adams, M. B. 1999. Acidic deposition and sustainable forest management in the central Appalachians, USA. For. Ecol. Manage. 122:17–28.

Ammer, F. K. 2003. Population level dynamics of grasshopper sparrow populations breeding on reclaimed mountaintop mines in West Virginia. Ph.D. dissertation. West Virginia University. Morgantown. Available at: https://eidr.wvu.edu/eidr/documentdata.eIDR?documentid=3242.

Anderson, J. M. 1991. The effect of climate change on decomposition processes of grasssland and foreal forests. Ecolo. Appl. 1:326–347.

Appenzeller, C., and T. F. Stocker. 1998. North Atlantic Oscillation dynamics recorded in Greenland ice cores. Science 282:446-449.

Arway, J. A. 1999. Overview: water pollution in Pennsylvania. A watershed primer for Pennsylvania. W. H. J. Woodwell, Pennsylvania Environmental Council, Allegheny Watershed Network and PA Department of Environmental Protection. 172 pp.

Askins, R. A., J. F. Lynch, and R. Greenberg. 1990. Population declines in migratory birds in eastern North America. Current Ornithology 7:1–57.

Askins, R. A., and M. J. Philbrick. 1987. Effects of changes in regional forest abundance on the decline and recovery of a forest bird community. Wilson Bulletin 99:7–21.

Bailey, R. G. (comp.). 1995. Description of the ecoregions of the United States. USDA For. Ser. Misc. Pub. 1391.

Baker, J. P., and C. L. Schofield. 1982. Aluminum toxicity to fish in acidic waters. Water Air and Soil Pollution 18:289–309.

Barden, L. S. 1981. Forest development in canopy gaps of a diverse hardwood forest of the southern Appalachian mountains. Oikos 37:205–209.

Barnes, B. V. 1991. Deciduous forest of North America. *In* E. Rohrig and B. Ulrich (eds.). Ecosystems of the world, temperate deciduous forests. Vol. 7. Elsevier, NY.

Barnes, B. V., D. R. Zak, S. R. Denton, and S. H. Spurr. 1998. Forest Ecology. 4th ed. John Wiley and Sons. NY.

Barr, M. W. 2002. Eastern hemlock (*Tsuga canadensis*) mortality in Shenandoah National Park. *In* Proceedings: Hemlock woolly adelgid in the eastern United States Symposium. February 5–7, 2002. East Brunswick, NJ.

Bengston, D. N., R. S. Potts, D. P. Fan, and E. G. Goetz. 2005. An analysis of the public discourse about urban sprawl in the United States: monitoring concern about a major threat to forests. For. Pol. Econ. 7:745–756.

Berz, G. A. 1993. Global warming and the insurance industry. Interdisciplinary Science Reviews 18:120–125.

Bissonette, J. A., and I. Storch. 2002. Fragmentation: is the message clear? Conservation Ecology 6:14–18.

Blaney, C., and J. A. Miller. 1995. Rooting for causes of succession. BioScience 45:741.

Bobbink, R., M. Hornung, and J. G. Roelofs. 1998. The effects of air-borne nitrogen pollutants on species diversity in natural and semi-natural European vegetation. J. Ecol. 86:717–738.

Boerner, R. E. 1984. Nutrient fluxes in litterfall and decomposition in four forests along a gradient of soil fertility in southern Ohio. Can. J. For. Res. 14:794–802.

Bonnicksen, T.M. 2000. America's ancient forests: from the ice age to the age of discovery. John Wiley & Sons. New York, NY.

Booth, D. B., and C. R. Jackson. 1997. Urbanization of aquatic systems: degradation threshold, stormwater detection, and the limits of mitigation. J. Amer. Water Res. Assn. 33:1077–1090.

Botkin, D. B., J. F. Janak, and J. R. Wallis. 1972. Rationale, limitations, and assumptions of a northeastern forest growth simulator. IBM J. Res. Dev. 16:101–116.

Bradford, D. F., S. E. Franson, A. C. Neale, D. T. Heggem, G. R. Miller, and G. E. Canterbury. 1998. Bird species assemblages as indicators of biological integrity in Great Basin rangeland. Env. Monitor. Assess. 49:1–22.

Bradley, N. L., A. C. Leopold, J. Ross, and W. Huffaker. 1999. Phenological changes reflect climate change in Wisconsin. Proc. Natl. Acad. Sci. USA. 96:9701–9704.

Bradt, P. 1994. Acid Precipitation and Surface Water Acidification: Implications for Aquatic Biodiversity. *In* Biological Diversity: Problems and Challenges. E. Miller, Pennsylvania Academy of Science.

Braun, E. L. 1950. Deciduous forests of eastern North America. Blakiston Co. Philadelphia, PA.

Breshears, D. D., and C. D. Allen. 2002. The importance of rapid, disturbance-induced losses in carbon management and sequestration. Global Ecology & Biogeography 11:1–5.

Brooks, M. L., C. M. D'Antonio, D. M. Richardson, J. G. Grace, J. E. Keeley, J. M. DiTomaso, R. J. Hobbs, M. Pellant, and D. Pyke. 2004. Effects of invasive plants on fire regimes. BioScience 54:677-688.

Brose, P. H., and T. A. Waldrop. 2000. Using prescribed fire to regenerate Table Mountain pine in the southern Appalachian Mountains. Pages 191–196 *In* W. K. Moser and C. F. Moser (eds.), Fire and forest ecology: innovative Silviculture and vegetation management. Tall Timbers Fire Ecology Conference Proceedings, No. 21. Tall Timbers Research Station. Tallahasee, FL.

Buell, M. F., H. F. Buell, and J. A. Small. 1954. Fire in the history of Mettler's Woods. Bull. Torrey Bot. Club 81:253–255.

Caley, M. J., K. A. Buckley, and G. P. Jones. 2001. Separating ecological effects of habitat fragmentation, degradation, and loss on coral comensals. Ecology 82:3435–3448.

Chapin, F. S. III. 1993. Functional role of growth forms in ecosystem and global processes. Pp. 287–312 *In* J. R. Ehleringer and C. B. Field, eds. Scaling physiological processes: leaf to globe. Academic Press. San Diego, CA.

Chapin, F. S., III, and G. R. Shaver. 1985. Individualistic growth response of tundra plant species to environmental manipulations in the field. Ecology 66:564–576.

Chapin, F. S., and G. Whiteman. 1998. Sustainable development of the boreal forest: interaction of ecological, social, and business feedbacks. Conservation Ecology 2:12.

Chapin, F. S., III, M. S. Torn, and M. Taneo. 1996. Principles of ecosystem sustainability. The American Naturalist 148:1016–1037.

Chappelka A. H., and B. I. Chevone. 1992. Tree responses to ozone. Pp. 271–334 *In* Leforn, A. S. ed. Surface level ozone exposures and their effects on vegetation. Lewis Publishers. Chelsea, MI.

Chappelka, A. H., and L. J. Samuelson. 1998. Ambient ozone effects on forest trees of the eastern United States: a review. New Phytologist 139:91–108.

Cheah, C. A. S-J., M. A. Mayer, D. Palmer, T. Scudder, and R. Chianese. 2005. Assessments of biological control of HWA with *Sasajiscymnus tsugae* in Connecticut and New Jersey. *In* Onken, B. and R. Reardon, comps. Proceedings, third symposium on hemlock woolly adelid in the eastern United States. USDA Forest Service FHTET-2005-1.

Clebsch, E. C., and R. T. Busing. 1989. Secondary succession, gap dynamics, and community structure in a southern Appalachian cove forest. Ecology 70:728–735.

Clutter, J. R. 1963. Compatible growth and yield models for loblolly pine. For. Sci. 9:354–371.

Collinge, S. K., and R. T. Foreman. 1998. A conceptual model of land conversion processes: predictions and evidence from a microlandscape experiment with grassland insects. Oikos: 82:66–84.

Comer, P., D. Faber-Langendoen, R. Evans, S. Gawler, C. Josse, G. Kittel, S. Menard, M. Pyne, M. Reid, K. Schulz, and others. 2003. Ecological systems of the United States: a working classification of the US terrestrial systems. NatureServe. Arlington, VA.

Conner, R. N., and J. G. Dickson. 1997. Relationships between bird communities and forest age, structure, species composition and fragmentation in the West Gulf Coastal Plain. Texas Journal of Science 49:123–138.

Cook, E. R., and G. C. Jacoby, Jr. 1977. Tree-ring-drought relationships in the Hudson Valley, New York. Science 198:399–401.

Core, E. L. 1966. The vegetation of West Virginia. McClain Printing Co. Parsons, WV.

Cronan, C. S., and D. F. Grigal. 1995. Use of calcium/aluminum ratios as indictors of stress in forest ecosystems. J. E. Q. 24:209–140.

Crow, T. R. 1988. Reproductive mode and mechanisms for self-replacement of northern red oak (*Quercus rubra*): a review. For. Sci. 34:19–40.

Dale, M. E. 1972. Growth and yield prdicitions for upland oak stands 10 years after thinning. USDA Forest Service, Res. Pap. NE-112.

Dale, V. H., L. A. Jouce, S. McNulty, R. P. Neilson, M. P. Ayres, M. D. Flannigan, P. J. Hanson, L. C. Irland, A. E. Lugo, C. J. Peterson, and others. 2001. Climate change and forest disturbances. BioScience 51:723–734.

D'Antonio, C. M, and P. M Vitousek 1992. Biological invasions by exotic grasses, the grass/fire cycle, and global change. Annual Review of Ecological Systematics 1992. 23:63–87

Davis, M. B. 1981. Quaternary history and the stability of forest communities. Chapter 10 *In* D. C. West, H. H. Shugart, and D. B. Botkin, eds. Forest succession. Springer-Verlag. New York, NY.

Dawson, T. E. 1993. Hydraulic life and water use by plants: implications for water balance, performance and plant-plant interactions. Oecologic 95:565–574.

DeAngelis, D. L., and W. M. Post. 1991. Positive feedback and ecosystem organization. Pp. 155–178 *In* M. Higashi and T. P. Burns, eds. Theoretical studies of ecosystems: the network perspective. Cambridge University Press. Cambridge.

Debinski, D. M., and R. D. Holt. 2000. A survey and overview of habitat fragmentation experiments. Conservation Biology 14:342–355.

DeCalesta, D. S. 1994. Effect of white-tailed deer on songbirds within managed forests in Pennsylvania. Journal of Wildlife Management 58:711–717.

DeHaynes, D. H., P. G. Schaberg, G. J. Hawley, and G. R. Stimbeck. 1999. Acid rain impacts calcium nutrition and forest health. BioScience 49:789–800.

Delcourt, H. R. 1987. The impact of prehistoric agriculture and land occupation on natural vegetation. TREE 2:39–44.

Delcourt, H. R., and P. A. Delcourt. 1998. Pre-Columbian native American use of fire on southern Appalachian landscapes. Conservation Biology 11:1010–1014.

Delcourt, P. A., and H. R. Delcourt. 1987. Long-term forest dynamics of the temperate zone. Springer-Verlag. New York, NY.

Demchik, M. C., and W. E. Sharpe. 2004. Litter decomposition in low and high mortality northern red oak stands on extremely acidic southwestern Pennsylvania soils. USDA Forest Service. Gen. Tech. Rep. SRS-73.

Denslow, J. S. 1980. Patterns of plant species diversity during succession under different disturbance regimes. Oecologia 46:18–21.

Denslow, J. S. 1985. Disturbance-mediated coexistence of species. Pp. 307–324 *In* S. T. A. Pickett, P.S. White (eds.), The ecology of natural disturbance and patch dynamics. Academic Press. New York, NY.

Dessecker, D. R., and H. Y. Richard. 1984. Songbird response to reproduction stocking levels in clearcut northern hardwood stands. Trans. Northeat Sec. Wildl. Soc. 41:181 (abstract only).

Dessecker, D. R., and H. Y. Richard. 1987. Breeding-bird communities associated with Pennsylvania northern hardwood clearcut stands. Proc. Pa. Acad. Sci. 61:170–173.

DeWalle, D. R., W. E. Sharpe, et al. 1982. Causes of acidification of four streams on Laurel Hill in southwestern Pennsylvania. Report OWRT-B-117-PA(2).

Diffendorder, J. E., M. S. Gaines, and R. D. Holt. 1995. The effects of habitat fragmentation on movements of three small mammal species. Ecology 76:827–839.

Driscoll, C. T., G. B. Lawrence, A. J. Bulger, T. J. Butler, C. S. Cronan, C. Eagar, K. F. Lambert, G. E. Likens, J. L. Stoddard, and K. C. Weathers. 2001. Acidic deposition in the northeastern United States: sources and inputs, ecosystem effects, and management strategies. BioScience 51:180–198.

Drohan, J. R., and W. E. Sharpe. 1997. Long-term changes in forest soil acidity in Pennsylvania, USA. Water Air and Soil Pollution 95:299–311.

Duchesne, L. C. and B. C. Hawkes. 2000. Fire in northern ecosystems. Chapter 3 *In* J. K. Brown and J. K. Smith, eds. Wildland fire in ecosystems: effects of fire on flora. USDA Forest Service. Gen. Tech. Rep. RMRS-42 Vol. 2.

Dunson, W. A. and R. L. Wyman. 1992. A symposium on amphibian declines and habitat acidification. Journal of Herpetology. University Park, PA.

Edwards, P., C. Huber, and F. Wood. 2004. Ozone exposures and implications for vegetation in rural areas of the central Appalachian Mountains, USA. Environmental Monitoring and Assessment 98:157–174.

Engleman, C. J. and W. F. McDiffett. 1996. Accumulation of aluminum and iron by bryophytes in streams affected by acid-mine drainage. Environmental Pollution 94:67–74.

Eschtruth, A., N. Cleavitt, J. J. Battles, and T. J. Fahey. Vegetation dynamics in declining hemlock stands in the Delaware Water Gap National Recreation Area: 9 years of forest response to hemlock woolly adelgid infestation.

Evans, R. A. 2003. Hemlock ecosystems and hemlock woolly adelgid at Delaware Water Gap National Recreation Area. Available from: http://na.fs.fed.us/fhp/hwa/pub/HemRpt03_USFS_website.pdf.

Evans, R. A. Hemlock ravines at Delaware Water Gap National Recreation Area: Highly valued, distinctive, and threatened ecosystems. *In* Delaware Water Gap National Recreation Area 30th Anniversary symposium. Available from Richard Evans, NPS, Delaware Water Gap National Recreation Area, 294 Old Milford Rd, Milford, PA 18337.

Falkengren-Grerup, U. 1993. Effects on beech forest species of experimentally enhanced nitrogen deposition. Flora 188:85–91.

Federer, C. A, J. W. Hornbeck, L. M. Tritton, C. W. Martin, R. S. Pierce, and C. T. Smith, 1989. Long-term depletion of calcium and other nutrients in eastern U. S. Forests. Environ. Manage. 13:593–601.

Fenneman, N. M. 1938. Physiography of the eastern United States. McGraw-Hill. New York, NY.

Fitter, A. H., A. Hodge, and T. J. Daniell. 1999. Resource sharing in plant-fungus communities: did the carbon move for you? TREE 14:70.

Fleming, K. K., and W. M. Giuliano. 2001. Reduced predation of artificial nests in border-edge cuts on woodlots. J. Wildl. Manage. 65:351–355.

Flowerdew, J. R., and S. A. Ellwood. 2001. Impacats of woodland deer on small mammal ecology. Forestry 74:277–287.

Foley, J. A., J. E. Kutzbach, M. T. Coe, and S. Levis. 1994. Feedbacks between climate and boreal forests during the Holocene epoch. Nature 371:52–54.

Fortney, R. H., S. L. Stephenson, and H. S. Adams. 1995. Reconnaissance vegetation study of the Bluestone, New, and Gauley River Gorges. Pp. 42–50 In Proceedings of the New River Symposium. April 7–8, 1995. Daniels, WV.

Franklin, J. F., H. H. Shugart, and M. E. Harmon. 1987. Tree death as an ecological process. BioScience 37:550–556.

Freda, J., and W. A. Dunson. 1985. The effect of acidic precipitation on amphibian breeding in temporary ponds in Pennsylvania. U.S. Fish and Wildlife Service. Biological Report. 80.

Freda, J., and W. A. Dunson. 1986. Effects of low pH and other chemical variables on the local distribution of amphibians. Copeia 2: 454–466.

Fredericksen, T. S. 1998. Impacts of logging and development on central Appalachian forests. N.A.J. 18:175–178.

Frelich, L. E., and C. G. Lorimer. 1985. Current and predicted long-term effects of deer browsing in hemlock forests in Michigan, USA. Biol. Conserv. 34:99–120.

Fritts, H. C. 1976. Tree rings and climate. Academic Press. New York, NY.

Frost, C. C. 1998. Presettlement fire frequency regimes of the United States: a first approximation. Pages 70–81 In T. L. Pruden and L. A. Brennan, eds. Fire in ecosystem management: shifting the paradigm from suppression to prescription. Tall Timbers Fire Ecology Conference Proceedings, No. 20. Tall Timbers Research Station. Tallahassee, FL.

Galatowitsch, S. M., N. O. Anderson, and P. D. Ascher. 1999. Invasiveness in wetland plants in temperate North America. Wetlands 19:733–755.

Gleason, H. A. 1917. The structure and development of the plant association. Bulletin of the Torrey Botanical Club 44:463–481.

Gleason, H. A. 1926. The individualistic concept of the plant association. Bulletin of the Torrey Botanical Club 53:7–26.

Goodale, C. L., and J. D. Aber. 2001. The long-term effects of land use history on nitrogen cycling in northern hardwood forests. Ecolo. Appl. 11:253–267.

Gough, L., and J. B. Grace. 1998. Herbivore effects on plant species density at varying productivity levels. Ecology 79:1586–1594.

Grafton, W. N. 1982. Plants and vegetation of the New River Gorge. Pp. 69–74. *In* Proceedings of the New River Symposium. May 6–8, 1982. Beckley, WV. Quality Printing Company. Sutton, WV.

Grafton, W. N. 1993. Vascular flora on the lower sections of Gauley, Meadow, and Bluestone Rivers. Pp. 123–134. *In* Proceedings of the New River Symposium. April 15–17. Wytheville, VA.

Guyette, R. P., and D. C. Dey. 2000. Humans, topography, and wildland fire: The ingredients for long-term patterns in ecosystems. Pp. 28–35. *In* Proceeding: Workshop on Fire, People, and the Central Hardwoods Landscape. USDA Forest Service. Gen. Tech. Rep. NE-274.

Haack, R. A., and J. W. Byler. 1993. Insects and pathogens: regulators of forest ecosystems. J. For. 91(9):32–37.

Haack, R. A. 1994. Insect-pollinated trees and shrubs in North America. Mich. Ent. Soc. Newsletter 39:8–9.

Haddad, N. M. 1999. Corridor and distance effects on interpatch movements: a landscape experiment with butterflies. Ecolo. Appl. 9:612–622.

Hairston, N. G., F. E. Smith, and L. B. Slobodkin. 1960. Community structure, population control and competition. American Naturalist 94:421–425.

Hanson, A. J., R. P. Neilson, V. H. Dale, C. H. Flather, L. R. Iverson, D. J. Currie, S. Shafer, R. Cook, and P. J. Bartlein. 2001. Global change in forests: responses of species, communities, and biomes. BioScience 51:765–779.

Helvey, J. D., and S. H. Kunkle. 1986. Input-output budgets of selected nutrients on an experimental watershed near Parsons, WV. Res. Pap. NE-584. USDA Forest Service. Northeastern Experiment Station. Broomall, PA.

Hersteinsson, P., and D. W. MacDonald. 1992. Interspecific competition and the geographical distribution of red and artic foxes *Vulpes* vulpes and *Alopex lagopus*. Oikos 64:505–515.

Hession. W. C., T. E. Johnson, D. F. Charles, D. D. Hart, R. J. Horwitz, D. A. Kreeger, J. E. Pizzuto, D. J. Velinsky, J. D. Newbold, C. Cianfrani, and others. 2000. Ecological benefits of riparian reforestation in urban watersheds: study design and preliminary results. Environ. Mon. Assess. 63:211–222.

Hicks, R. R., Jr., and P. S. Frank, Jr. 1984. Relationship of aspect to soil nutrients, species importance, and biomass in a forested watershed in West Virginia. For. Ecol. Manage. 8:281–291.

Hicks, R. R., Jr., S. Maxwell, and J. Rentch. 2005. Vital signs assessment: preliminary short list for terrestrial systems, Eastern Rivers and Mountains Network. Unpublished monograph.

Hobbie, S. E. 1992. Effects of plant species on nutrient cycling. TREE 7:336–339.

Hobbs, N. T. 1996. Modification of ecosystems by ungulates. J. Wildl. Manage. 60:695–713.

Hobbs, R. J, and L. F. Huenneke. 1992. Disturbance, diversity, and invasion: implications for conservation. Conservation Biology 6:324–337.

Holling, C. S. 1992. The role of forest insects in structuring the boreal landscape. Pages 170–191 *In* H. H. Shugart, R. Leemans, and G. B. Bonan, eds. A systems analysis of the global boreal forest. Cambridge University Press. Cambridge, UK.

Holt, R., G. R. Robinson, and M. S. Gaines. 1995. Vegetation dynamics in an experimentally fragmented landscape. Ecology 76:1610–1624.

Hoover, J. P., M. C. Brittingham and L. J. Goodrich. 1995. Effects of forest patch size on nesting success of wood thrushes. The Auk 112(1):146-155.

Horne, M. T., and W. A. Dunson. 1994. Exclusion of the Jefferson salamander from some potential breeding ponds in Pennsylvania: Effects of pH, temperature and metals on embryonic development. Archives of Environmental Contamination and Toxicology. 27:323–330.

Horne, M. T., and W. A. Dunson. 1995. Toxicity of metals and low pH to embryos and larvae of the Jefferson Salamander. Archives of Environmental Contamination and Toxicology 29:110–114.

Horsley, S. B., R. P. Long, S. W. Bailey, R. A. Hallet, and T. J. Hall. 1999. Factors contributing to sugar maple decline along topographic gradients on the glaciated and unglaciated Appalachian Plateau. Pp 60–62 *In* S. B. Horsley and R. P. Long, eds. Sugar maple ecology and health: proceedings of an International Symposium. USDA Forest Service. Gen. Tech. Rep. NE-261.

Horsley, S. B., S. L. Stout, and D. S. DeCalesta. 2003. White-tailed deer impact on the vegetation dynamics of a northern hardwood forest. Ecological Applications 13:98–118.

Houghton, J. T, Y. Ding, D. J. Griggs, M. Noguer, P. J. van der Linden, X. Dai, K. Maskell, and C. A. Johnson. 2001. *In* Climate change 2001: The scientific basis. Contribution of working group 1 to the Third Assessment Report of the Intergovernmental Panel on Climate Change. Cambridge University Press. Cambridge.

Hunt, D. M., and R.E. Zaremba. 1992. The northeastward spread of *Microstegium vimineum* (Poaceae) into New York and adjacent states. Rhodora 94:167–170.

Hunter, M. L. 1996. Benchmarks for managing ecosystems: are human activities natural? Conservation Biology 10:695–697.

Irland, L. C., D. Adams, R. Alig, C. J. Betz, C. Chen, M. Hutchins, B. A. McCarl, K. Skog, and B. L. Sohngen. 2001. Assessing socioeconomic impacts of climate change on US forests, wood-product markets, and forest recreation. BioScience 51:753–764.

Iverson, L. R. 2002. Biological trends in the United States: an annotated on-line review. http://www.fs.fed.us/ne/delaware/biotrends/biotrends.html

Iverson, L. R., A. M. Prasad, B. J. Hale, and E. K. Sutherland. 1999. Atlas of current and potential future distributions of common trees of the eastern United States. USDA For. Ser. Gen. Tech. Rep. NE-265.

Iverson, L. R., M. W. Schwartz, and A. M. Prasad. 2004. Potential colonization of newly available tree species habitat under climate change: an analysis for five eastern species. Landscape Ecology 19:787–799.

Jacobi, J. C., and F. H. Tainter. 1988. Dendroclimatic examination of white oak along an environmental gradient in the Piedmont of South Carolina. Castanea 53:252–262.

Janzen, F. J. 1994. Climate-change and temperature-dependent sex determination in reptiles. Proc. Natl. Acad. Sci. USA 91:7484–7490.

Jenkins, J. C., J. D. Aber, and C. D. Canham. 1999. Hemlock woolly adelgid impacts on community structure and N cycling rates in eastern hemlock forests. Can. J. For. Res. 29:630–645.

Jenny, H. 1941. Factors of soil formation: a system of quantitative pedology. McGraw-Hill. New York, NY.

Jenny, H. 1980. The soil resource: origin and behavior. Springer-Verlag. New York, NY.

Johnson, D. W., D. D. Richter, G. M. Lovett, and S. E. Lindberg. 1985. The effects of atmospheric deposition on potassium, calcium, and magnesium cycling in two deciduous forests. Can. J. For. Res. 15:773–782.

Kareiva, P. 1987. Habitat fragmentation and the stability of predator prey interactions. Nature 26:388–390.

Karl, T. R., R. W. Knight, D. R. Easterling, and R. G. Quayle. 1995. Indices of climate change for the United States. Bull. Am. Meteor. Soc. 77:279–292.

Keller, W., and J. M. Gunn. 1995. Lake water quality improvements and recovering aquatic communities. Pp. 67–80 *In* J. M. Gunn, ed. Restoration and recovery of an industrial region: progress in restoring the smelter-damaged landscape near Sudbury, Canada. Springer-Verlapg. New York, NY.

Kimmel W. G., E. L. Cooper, and C. C. Wagner. 1996. Macroinvertebrate and fish populations of four streams receiving high rates of hydrogen and sulfate ion deposition. Journal of Freshwater Ecology 11:493–511.

Kram, P. S., R. C. Santore, C. T. Driscoll, J. D. Aber, and J. Hruska. 1999. Application of the forest-soil-water model (PneET-BGC/CHESS) to the Lysina catchment, Czech Republic. Ecological Modelling 120:9–30.

Kremen, C., R. K. Colwell, T. L. Erwin, D. D. Murphy, R. F. Noss, and M. A. Sanjayan. 1993. Terrestrial arthropod assemblages: their use in conservation planning. Conservation Biology 7:796–807.

Kuchler, A. W. 1964. Potential natural vegetation of the conterminous United States (map and manual). American Geographical Society, Special Publication Number 36.

Landres, P. B., J. Verner, and J. W. Thomas. 1988. Ecological uses of vertebrate indicator species: a critique. Conservation Biology 4:316–328.

Landres, P. B., P. Morgan, and F. J. Swanson. 1999. Overview of the use of natural variability concepts in managing ecologic systems. Ecolo. Appl. 9:1179–1188.

Laurance, W. F., L. V. Ferreira, J. M. Rankin-de Merona, S. G. Laurance, R. W. Hutchings, and T. E. Lovejoy. 1998. Effects of forest fragmentation on recruitment patterns in Amazonian tree communities. Conservation Biology 12:460–464.

Lawrence, G. B., M. B. David, and W. C. Shortle. 1995. A new mechanism for calcium loss in forest-floor soils. Nature 378:162–164.

Lawrence, G. B., and T. G. Huntington. 1999. Soil calcium depletion linked to acid rain and forest growth in the eastern United States. U.S. Geological Survey, Information Services. Available at http://water.usgs.gov.

Leblanc, D. C., and Foster, J. R. 1992. Predicting effects of global warming on growth and mortality of upland oak species in the midwestern United States: a physiologically based dendroecological approach. Can. J. For. Res. 22:1739–1752.

Liebhold, A. M., W. L. McDonald, D. Bergdahl, and V. C. Mastro. 1995. Invasion by exotic pests: a threat to forest ecosystems. For. Sci Monograph 30:1–49.

Likens, G. E., T. J. Butler, and D. C. Buso. 2001. Long- and short-term changes in sulfate deposition: effects of the 1990 Clean Air Act Amendments. Biogeochemistry 41:89–173.

Long, R. P., S. B. Horsley, and P. R. Lilja. 1997. Impact of forest liming on growth and crown vigor of sugar maple and associated hardwoods. Can. J. For. Res. 27:1560–1573.

Lynch, J. A., and E. S. Corbett. 1980. Acid precipitation - a threat to aquatic ecosystems. Fisheries 5:8–12.

Lynch, J., K. Horner, et al. 2000. Atmospheric deposition: spatial and temporal variations in Pennsylvania. Report to the Pennsylvania Department of Environmental Protection.

MacArthur, R. H., and E. O. Wilson. 1967. The theory of island biogeography. Princeton University Press. Princeton, N.J.

MacInnes, C. D., E. H. Dunn, D. H. Rusch, F. Cooke, and F. G. Cooch. 1990. Advancement of goose nesting dates in the Hudson Bay Region, 1951–86. Canadian Field Naturalist 104:295–297.

Mack, R. N., D. Simberloff, W. M. Lonsdale, H. Evans, M. Clout, and F. Bazzaz. 2000. Biotic invasions: causes, epidemiology, global consequences, and control. Ecol. Appl. 10:689–710.

Mahan, C. G. 2004. A Natural Resource Assessment for New River Gorge National River. Natural Resource Report NPA/NERCHAL/NRR-04/006. U.S. Department of Interior. National Park Service. Northeast Region. Philadelphia, PA.

Mahan, C. G., and R. H. Yahner. 1996. Effects of forest fragmentation on burrow-site selection by eastern chipmunk (*Tamias striatus*). Amer. Midl. Nat. 136:352–357.

Mahan, C. G., and R. H. Yahner. 1999. Effects of forest fragmentation on behavior patterns in the eastern chipmunk (*Tamias striatus*). Can. J. Zoo. 77:1991–1997.

Malcolm, J. R., A. Markham, R. P. Neilson, and M. Garaci. 2002. Estimated migration rates under scenarios of global climate change. J. Biogeo. 29:835–849.

Mallet, J. 2005. Hybridization as an invasion of the genome. TREE 20:229–237.

Mann, W., P. Dorn, and R. Brandl. 1991. Local distribution of amphibians: the importance of habitat fragmentation. Global Ecology and Biogeography Letters 1:36–41.

Manville, G. C., and H. J. Webster. 1998. Bryophytes and lichens: review status in Pennsylvania. *In* Yahner, R. H., ed. Inventory and Monitoring of Biotic Resources in Pennsylvania. Pennsylvania Biological Survey. Harrisburg, PA.

Marquis, D. A. 1974. The impact of deer browing on Allegheny hardwood regeneration. USDA Forest Service Res. Pap. NE-57.

Marquis, D. A. 1981. Effect of deer browing on timber producing in Allegheny hardwood forests of northwestern Pennsylvania. USDA Forest Service, Res. Pap. NE-475.

Marquis, D. A., and R. Brenneman. 1981. The impact of deer on forest vegetation in Pennsylvania. USDA Forest Service. Gen. Tech. Rep. NE-65.

Marshall, M., and N. Piekielek. 2004. Long-term ecological monitoring program, Phase 1 report. (draft). Eastern Rivers and Mountains Network. USDI National Park Service. University Park, PA.

Mattson, W. J., and N. D. Addy. 1975. Phytophagous insects as regulators of forest primary productivity. Science 190:515–522.

McCabe, G. J., M. A. Palecki, and J. L. Betancourt. 2004. Pacific and Atlantic Ocean influences on multidecadal drought frequency in the United States. PNAS 101:4136–4141.

McCarthy, B. C., C. J. Small, and D. L. Rubino. 2001. Composition, structure and dynamics of Dysart Woods, an old-growth mixed mesophytic forest of southeastern Ohio. For. Ecol. Manage. 140:193–213.

McGarigal, K., and S. Cushman. 2002. Comparative evaluation of experimental approaches to the study of habitat fragmentation. Ecological Applications 12:335–345.

McGraw, J. B., and M. A. Furedi. 2005. Deer browsing and population viability of a forest understory plant. Science 307:920–922.

McGuire, A.D., I. C. Prentice, N. Ramankutty, T. Reichenau, A. Schloss, H. Tian, L. J. Williams, and U. Wittenberg. 2001. Carbon balance of the terrestrial biosphere in the twentieth century: Analyses of CO_2, climate and land use effects with four process-based ecosystem models. Global Biogeochemical Cycles 15:183–192.

McLaughlin, S. B., C. P. Anderson, P. J. Hanson, M. G. Tjoelker, and W. K. Roy. 1991. Increased dark respiration and calcium deficiency of red spruce in relation to acid deposition at high-elevation southern Appalachian Mountain sites. Can. J. For. Res. 21:1234–1244.

McShea, W.J., and J. H. Rappole. 2000. Managing the abundance and diversity of breeding bird populations through manipulation of deer populations. Conservation Biology 14:1161–1170.

Meffe, G. K., and C. R. Carroll. 1997. Principles of conservation biology. 2nd ed. Sinauer Associates, Inc. Sunderland, MA.

Mikusinski, G., M. Gromadzki, and P. Chylarecki. 2001. Woodpeckers as indicators of forest bird diversity. Conservation Biology 15:208–217.

Morgan, P., G. H. Aplet, J. B. Haufler, H. C. Humphries, M. M. Moore, and W. D. Wilson. 1994. Historical range of variability: a useful tool for evaluating ecosystem change. J. Sus. For. 2:87–111.

Myers, W. L. and Irish. 1981. Vegetation survey of Delaware Water Gap National Recreation Area. Final Report. USDI, National Park Service, Mid-Atlantic Region. Available from Richard Evans, NPS, Delaware Water Gap National Recreation Area, 294 Old Milford Rd, Milford, PA 18337.

Nash, B. L., D. D. Davis, et al. 1992. Forest Health Along a Wet Sulfate/pH Deposition Gradient in North-Central Pennsylvania. Environmental Toxicology and Chemistry 11:1075–1104.

Norris, S. J. 1992. Rare species survey of Bluestone Scenic River, West Virginia. Natural Heritage Program, Division of Natural Resources, National Park.

Nowacki, G. J., and M. D. Abrams. 1997. Radial-growth averaging criteria for reconstructing disturbance histories from presettlement-origin oaks. Ecol. Monogr. 67:225–249.

O'Connell, T. J., L. E. Jackson, and R. P. Brooks. 2000. Bird guilds as indicators of ecological condition in the central Appalachians. Ecol. Appl. 10:1706–1721

Ojima, D. S., T. G. F. Kittel, T. Rosswall, and B. H. Walker. 1991. Critical issues for understanding global change effects on terrestrial ecosystems. Ecolo. Appl. 1:316–325.

Oksanen, L. 1990. Predation, herbivory, and plant strategies along gradients of primary productivity. Pp 445–474 *In* J. B. Grace and D. Tilman, eds. Perspectives on plant competition. Academic Press. San Diego, CA.

Oliver, C. D., and B. C. Larsen. 1996. Forest stand dynamics. John Wiley & Sons. New York, NY.

Orwig, D. A., and Abrams, M. D. 1997. Variation in radial growth responses to drought among species, site, and canopy strata. TREE 11:474–484.

Ottersen, G., B. Planque, A. Belgrano, E. Post, P. C. Reid, and N. C. Stenseth. 2001. Ecological effects of the North Atlantic Oscillation. Oecologia 128:1–14.

Pacala, S. W., C. D. Canham, and J. A. J. Silander. 1993. Forest models defined by field measurements: I. The design of a northeastern forest simulator. Can. J. For. Res. 23:1980–1988.

Pastor, J., R. J. Naiman, B. Dewey, and P. McInnes. 1988. Moose, microbes, and the boreal forest. BioScience 38:770–777.

Pennsylvania Department of Environmental Protection (PADEP). 2001. Water quality assessment 305(b) Report. PA Department of Environmental Protection, Bureau of Watershed Conservation. Harrisburg, PA.

Perry, D. A., M. P. Amaranthus, J. G. Borchers, S. L. Borchers, and R. E. Brainerd. 1989. Bootstrapping in ecosystems. BioScience 39:230–237.

Pettersson, R. P, J. P. Ball, K. Renhorn, P. Essen, and K. Sjoberg. 1995. Invertebrate communities in boreal forest canopies as influenced by forestry and lichens with implications for passerine birds. Biological Conservation 74:57–63.

Phipps, R. L. 1982. Comments on interpretation of climatic information from tree rings, eastern North America. Tree-Ring Bull. 42:11–22.

Pickett, S. T. A. and P. S. White, eds. 1985. The ecology of natural disturbance and patch dynamics. Academic Press. New York, NY.

Pimentel D., L. Lach, R. Zuniga, and D. Morrison. 1999. Environmental and economic costs associated with non-indigenous species in the United States. http://www.news.cornell.edu/releases/Jan99/species_costs.html (June 12, 1999).

Post, E., and N. C. Stenseth. 1999. Climatic variability, plant phenology, and northern ungulates. Ecology 80:1322–1339.

Prasad, A. M., and L. R. Iverson. A climate change atlas for 80 forest tree species of the eastern United States. [spatial database] USDA Forest Service. Available at http://www.fs.fed.us/ne/delaware/atlas/.

Pyne, S. 2001. The source. Address to Joint Conference of American Society for Environmental History and the Forest History Society. Available at http://www.lib.duke.edu/forest/Events/lecture2001.html.

Ranger, J., and M. P. Turpault. 1999. Input-output nutrient budgets as a diagnostic tool for sustainable forest management. For. Ecol. Manage. 122:139–154.

Read, D. 1997. The ties that bind. Nature 388:517–518.

Rentch, J. S., F. Desta, and G. W. Miller. 2002. Climate, canopy disturbance, and radial growth averaging in a second-growth mixed-oak forest in West Virginia, U.S.A. Can. J. For. Res. 32:915–927.

Rentch, J. S., M. A. Fajvan, and R. R. Hicks, Jr. 2003a. Spatial and temporal disturbance characteristics of oak-dominated old-growth stands in the central hardwood forest region. For. Sci. 49:778–789.

Rentch, J. S., M. A. Fajvan, and R. R. Hicks, Jr. 2003b. Oak establishment and canopy accession strategies in five old-growth stands in the central hardwood forest region. Forest Ecology and Management 184:285–297.

Rentch, J. S., R. H. Fortney, S. L. Stephenson, H. S. Adams, W. N. Grafton, R. B. Coxe, and H. H. Mills. (In press). Vegetation patterns within the lower Bluestone River Gorge in southern West Virginia. Castanea.

Rentch, J. S., and R. R. Hicks, Jr. 2000. Nutrient fluxes for two small forested watersheds: sixteen-year results from the West Virginia University Forest. WV Agricultural and Forestry Experiment Station. Rep.

Richardson, D. M., P. Pysek, M. Rejmanek, M. G. Barbour, F. D. Panetta, and C. J. West. 2000. Naturalization and invasion of alien plants: concepts and definitions. Diversity and Distributions 6:93–107.

Robbins, C. S., J. R. Saur, R. S. Greenberg, and S. Droge. 1989. Population declines in North American birds that migrate to the neotropics. Proceedings of the National Academy of Sciences of the USA 86:7658–7662.

Rodewald, P. G., and R. D. James. 1996. Yellow-throated Vireo (*Vireo flavifrons*). Number 247 *In* A. Poole and F. Gill, eds. The birds of North America. Academy of Natural Sciences. Philadelphia, Pa. And the American Ornithologists' Union. Washington, DC.

Romme, W. H., and W. M. Martin. 1982. Natural disturbance by tree-falls in an old-growth mixed mesophytic forest: Lilly Cornett Woods, Kentucky. *In* R. N. Muller, ed. Proceedings, 4th Central Hardwood Forest Conference. Univ. of Kentucky. Lexington.

Rooney, T. P., and D. M. Waller. 2001. How experimental defoliation and leaf height affect growth and reproduction in *Trillium grandiflorum*. J. Torrey Bot. Soc. 128:393–399.

Rooney, T. P., and D. M. Waller. 2003. Direct and indirect effects of white-tailed deer in forest ecosystems. Forest Ecology and Management 181:165–176.

Rooney, T. P., R. J. McCormick, S. L. Solheim, and D. M. Waller. 2002. Factors influencing the regeneration of northern white cedar in lowland forests of the Upper Great Lakes region, USA. For. Ecolo. Manage. 163:119–130.

Ross, R. M., L. A. Redell, and R. M. Bennett. 2002. Mesohabitat use of threatened hemlock forests by breeding birds of the Delaware Water Gap National Recreation Area. *In* Proceedings hemlock woolly adelgid in the eastern United States symposium. New Jersey Agricultural Experiment Station, Rutgers University. New Brunswick, NJ.

Rossell, C. R., Jr., B. Gorsira, and S. Patch. 2005. Effects of white-tailed deer on vegetation structure and woody seedling composition in three forest types on the Piedmont Plateau. For. Ecolo. Manage. 210:415–424.

Rowe, C., and W. Sadinski. 1992. Effects of acute and chronic acidification on three larval amphibians that breed in temporary ponds. Arch. Environmental Contamination and Toxicology 20:261–266.

Rubino, D. L., and B. C. McCarthy. 2000. Dendroclimatological analysis of white oak (*Quercus alba* L., Fagaceae) from an old-growth forest of southeastern Ohio, U.S.A. J. Torrey Bot. Soc. 127:240–250.

Ruffner, C. M., and M. D. Abrams. 1998. Lightning strikes and resultant fires from archival (1912–1917) and current (1960–1997) information in Pennsylvania. J. Torrey Bot. Soc. 125:249–252.

Runkle, J. R. 1982. Patterns of disturbance in some old-growth mesic forests of the eastern United States. Ecology 63:1533–1546.

Runkle, J. R. 1985. Disturbance regimes in temperate forests. Chapter 2 *In* S. T. A. Pickett and P. S. White, eds. The ecology of natural disturbance and patch dynamics. Academic Press. New York, NY.

Runkle, J. R. 1990. Gap dynamics in an Ohio *Acer-Fagus* forest and speculations on the geography of disturbance. Can. J. For. Res. 20:632–641.

Russell, F. L., D. B. Zippin, and N. L. Fowler. 2001. Effects of white-tailed deer (*Odocoileus virginianus*) on plants, plant populations and communities: a review. Am. Midl. Nat. 146:1–26.

Ryel, R. J., M. M. Caldwell, C. K. Yoder, D. Or, and A. J. Leffler. 2002. Hydraulic redistribution in a stand of *Artemsia tridentata*: evaluation of benefits to transpiration assessed with a simulative model. Oecologia 130:173–184.

Saunders, D. A, R. J. Hobbs, and C. R. Margules. 1991. Biological consequences of ecosystem fragmentation: a review. Biol. Conserve. 5:18–32.

Schlesinger, W. H. 1997. Biogeochemistry: an analysis of global change. 2nd ed. Academic Press. New York, NY.

Schmidt, K. M.; J. P..Menakis, C. C. Hardy,H. Colin, Wendel J.; D. L. Bunnell. 2002. Development of coarse-scale spatial data for wildland fire and fuel management. USDA Frest Service. Gen. Tech. Rep. RMRS-GTR-87. Available at www.fs.fed.us/fire/fuelman

Schneck, M., W. E. Sharpe, and J. Drohan. 1999. Acid Rain: the Pennsylvania connection. Penn State College of Agricultural Sciences, University Park, PA. (Available at: http://pubs.cas.psu.edu/FreePubs/pdfs/UH127.pdf).

Schoennagel, T., T. Veblen, and W. H. Romme. 2004. The interactyion of fire, fuels, and climate across the Rocky Mountain Forests. BioScience 54:661–676.

Scott, M. L., M. E. Miller, and J. C. Schmidt. 2005. The structure and functioning of riparian ecosystems of the Colorado Plateau—conceptual models to inform the vital sign selection process.

Sharpe, W. E. 1990. Impact of acid precipitation on Pennsylvania's aquatic biota: an overview. *In* Atmospheric deposition in Pennsylvania: a critical assessment. Environmental Resources Research Institute, University Park, PA. Environmental Resource Research Institute Publication. Pp. 98–107.

Sharpe, W. E., and M. C. Demchik. 1998. Acid runoff caused fish loss as an early warning of forest decline. Environmental Monitoring and Assessment 51:157–162.

Sharpe, W. E., T. G. Perlic, et al. 1987. Status of headwater benthic insect populations in an area of high hydrogen ion and sulfate deposition. Northeastern Environmental Science 6:23–30.

Sharpe, W. E., V. G. Leibfried, et al. 1987. The relationship of water quality and fish occurrence to soils and geology in an area of high hydrogen and sulfate ion deposition. Water Resources Bulletin 23:37–46.

Shortle, W. C., and K. T. Smith. 1988. Aluminum induced calcium deficiency syndrome in declining red spruce trees. Science 240:1017–1018.

Shortle, W. C., K. T. Smith, R. Mincocha, G. B. Lawrence, and M. B. David. 1997. Acid deposition, cation mobilization, and stress in healthy red spruce trees. J. Environ. Qual. 26:871–876.

Showman, R., and R. P. Long. 1992. Lichen studies along a wet sulfate deposition gradient in Pennsylvania. Bryologist 92:112–116.

Simard, S. W., M. D. Jones, D. M. Durall, D. A. Perry, D. D. Myold, and R. Molina. 1997a. Reciprocal transfer of carbon isotopes between ectomycorrhizal *Betula papyrifera* and *Psuedotsuga menziesii*. New Phytologist 137:529–542.

Simard, S. W., M. D. Jones, D. M. Durall, D. A. Perry, D. D. Myold, and R. Molina. 1997b. Net transfer of carbon between ectomycorrhizal tree species in the field. Nature 388:570–582.

Simberloff, D. 1986. Design of nature reserves. Pp. 315–337 *In* M. B. Usher, ed. Wildlife conservation evaluation. Chapman and Hall. London, UK.

Slobodkin, L. B. 2001. The good, the bad, and the reified. Evolutionary Ecology Research 3:1–13.

Sousa, W. P. 1984. The role of disturbance in natural communities. Ann. Rev. Ecol. Syst. 15:353–391.

Starfield, A. M., and F. S. Chapin, III. 1996. Model of transient changes in arctic and boreal vegetation in response to climate and land use change. Ecolo. Appl. 6:842–864.

Stephenson, S. L., A. N. Ash, and D. F. Stauffer. 1993. Appalachian oak forests. Chapter 6 *In* W. H. Martin, S. G. Boyce, and A. C. Echternacht, eds. Biodiversity of the southeastern United States: upland terrestrial communities. John Wiley & Sons. New York, NY.

Stevens, D. L. 1994. Implementation of a national monitoring program. J. Environ. Manage. 42:1–29.

Strausbaugh, P. D., and E. L. Core. 1977. Flora of West Virginia, second edition. Seneca Books. Grantsville, WV.

Sturm, M., C. Racine, and K. Tape. 2001. Increasing shrub abundance in the Artic. Nature 411:546–547.

Subak, S. 2006. The potential impacts of global warming on the Mid-Atlantic region. U.S. Global Change Research Program. http://www.climatehotmap.org/impacts/midatlantic.html.

Suiter, D. W., and D. K. Evans. 1995. Vascular flora of the New River Gorge National River, West Virginia rare species and plant migrations. Pp. 144–153 *in* Proceedings of the New River Symposium. April 7–8, 1996. Daniels, WV.

Sullivan, K., B. Black, C. Mahan, M. Abrams, K. C. Kim, and R. Yahner. 1998. Overstory tree composition of hemlock and hardwood stands in Delaware Water Gap National Recreation Area. Center for Biodiversity Research, Environmental Resources Research Institute, Pennsylvania State University. University Park, PA.

Sutherland, E. K. 1997. History of fire in a southern Ohio second-growth mixed oak forest. *In* S. G. Pallardy, R. A. Cecich, H. G. Garrett, and P. S. Johnson, eds. Proc. 11th central hardwood forest conference. USDA Forest Service. Gen Tech. Rep. NC-188.

Tajchman, S. J. 1983. Solar radiation climate of a forested catchment. West Virginia Forestry Notes. Circular 123. West Virginia Univ. Agricultural and Forestry Experiment Station. Morgantown, WV.

Taylor, G. E, D. W. Johnson, and C. P. Anderson. 1994. Air pollution and forest ecosystems: a regional to global perspective. Ecol. Appl. 4:662–689.

Templeton, A. R., K. Shaw, E. Routman, and S. K. Davis. 1990. The genetic consequences of habitat fragmentation. Ann. Missouri. Bot. Gard. 77:13–27.

The Nature Conservancy (TNC). 1996. Alien Invaders: America's Least Wanted. http://consci.tnc.org/li brary/pubs/dd/

The Nature Conservancy (TNC). 2000a. Map of U. S. ecoregions, based on Bailey (1994). Western Conservation Science Center. Available at: http://gis.tnc.org/data/MapbookWebsite/map_page.php?map_id=27

The Nature Conservancy (TNC). 2000b. Lower New England-Northern Piedmont Ecoregion Plan. Available at: http://conserveonline.org/docs/2005/03/LNEplanwithAppendices.pdf

The Nature Conservancy (TNC). 2001. Central Appalachian Forest Ecoregion Plan. Available at http://conserveonline.org/docs/2005/03/CAP-plan_2001.pdf

The Nature Conservancy (TNC). 2003. The Cumberlands and Southern Ridge and Valley Ecoregion: a plan for biodiversity conservation. Arlington, VA.

The Nature Conservancy (TNC). 2004. The High Allegheny Plateau (HAL) Ecoregion Plan. Available at http://conserveonline.org/docs/2005/03/HALplan.pdf

Thomas, C. D., and J. J. Lennon. 1999. Birds extend their ranges northwards. Nature 399:213.

Thornton, K.W., Holbrook, S.P., Stolte, K.L., and R. B. Landy. 2000. Effects of forest management practices on mid-Atlantic streams. Environment Monitoring and Assessment 63:31–41.

Tilman, D. 1988. Plant strategies and the dynamics and function of plant communities. Princeton University Press. Princeton, NJ.

Turner, M. G., et al. 1998. Factors influencing succession: lessons from large, infrequent natural disturbances. Ecosystems 1:511–523.

Ungerer, M. J., M. P. Ayres, and M. J. Lombardero. 1999. Climate and the norther distribution limits of *Dendroctonus frontalis* Zimmerman (Coleoptera:Scolytidae). J. Biogeo. 26:1133–1145.

U.S. Environmental Protection Agency (EPA). 1993. Natural wetlands and urban stormwater: potential impacts and management. Washington, DC. United States Environmental Protection Agency. 84 pp.

U.S. Environmental Protection Agency (EPA). 1996. Air quality criteria for ozone and related photochemical oxidants. EPA, Office of Air Quality Planning and Standards, Research Triangle Park, NC. EPA-600/P-93/004bF.

U.S. Environmental Protection Agency (EPA). 2001. How will climate change affect the mid-Atlantic Region? Washington, DC.

U.S.DOI, National Park Service. No date. NPS Inventory and monitoring program: introduction and background. Available at http://science.nature.nps.gov/im/monitor/index.htm.

U.S. DOI, National Park Service, Northeast Region. 2000. Environmental assessment for the release and establishment of *Pseudoscymnus tsugae* (Coleoptera: Coccinellideae) as a biological control agent for hemlock woolly adelgid (*Adelges tsugae*) at Delaware Water Gap National Recreation Area.

Vale, T. R. 1998. The myth of the humanized landscape: an example from Yosemite National Park. Nat. Areas J. 18:231–236.

Van Lear, D. H., and T. A. Waldrop. 1989. History, uses, and effects of fire in the Appalachians. USDA Forest Service. Gen. Tech. Rep. SE-54.

Vanderhorst, J. 2002. Two cliff top pine communities in the north section of New River Gorge National River, West Virginia. U.S. Department of Interior. National Park Service. New River Gorge National River. Glen Jean, WV.

Wade, D. D., B. L. Brock, P. H. Brose, J. B. Grace, G. A. Hock, and W. A. Patternson III. 2000. Fire in eastern ecosystems. Chapter 4 *In* Brown, J. K. and J. K. Smith, eds. Wildland fire in ecosystems: effects of fire on flora. USDA Forest Service. Gen. Tech. Rep. RMRS-42 Vol. 2.

Waldrop, T.A., Brose, P.H., Welch, N.T., Mohr, H.H., Gray, E.A., Tainter, F.H., and Ellis, L.E. 2003. Are crown fires necessary for table mountain pine? Pages 157–163 *In* K.E.M. Galley, R.C. Klinger, and N.G. Sugihara (eds.). Fire Conference 2000: The First National Congress on Fire Ecology, Prevention, and Management. Misc. Pub. No. 13. Tall Timbers Research Station. Tallahassee, FL.

Wallace, M. S., and F. P. Hain. 2000. Field surveys and evaluation of native and established predators of the hemlock woolly adelgid (Homoptera: Adelgidae) in the southeastern United States. Environ. Entomol. 29:638–644.

Waller, D. M., and W. S. Alverson. 1997. The white-tailed deer: a keystone herbivore. Wildl. Soc. Bull. 25:217–226.

Walther, G. R. 2000. Climatic forcing on the dispersal of exotic species. Phytoeoenologia 30:409–430.

Walther, G. R., C. A. Burga, and P. J. Edwards (eds.). 2001. "Fingerprints" of climate change— adapted behavior and shifting species ranges. Kluwer Academic/Pelennum. New York, NY.

Wang, D., and F. H. Bormann. 1986. Regional tree growth reductions due to ambient ozone: evidence from field experiments. Environment, Science and Technology 20:1122–1125.

Waring, R. H., and S. T. Running. 1998. Forest ecosystems: Analysis at multiple scales. 2nd ed. Academic Press. New York, NY.

Watts, W. A. 1979. Late Quaternary vegetation of central Appalachia and the New Jersey coastal plain. Ecolo. Monogr. 49:427–469.

Weir, D. N., and J. G. Greis. 2002. The southern forest resource assessment. USDA Forest Service, Gen. Tech. Rep. SRS-53.

White, P. S., J. Harrod, W. H. Romme, and J. L. Betancourt. 1999. Disturbance and temporal dynamics. Pp. 566–584 *In* R. C. Szaro, N. C. Johnson, W. T. Sexton, and A. J. Malk, eds. Ecological stewardship: A common reference for ecosystem management, Vol II. Elsevier Science Ltd. Oxford, UK.

Wigington, P. J., Jr., J. P. Baker, et al. 1996. Episodic acidification of small streams in the northeastern United States: Episodic response project. Ecological Applications 6:374–388.

Wilcove, D. S., D. Rothstein, J. Dubow, A. Phillips, and E. Losos. 1998. Quantifying threats to imperiled species in the United States: assessing the relative importance of habitat destruction, alien species, pollution, overexploitation, and disease. BioScience 48:607–615.

Wilkinson, D. M. 1998. The evolutionary ecology of mycorrhizal networks. Oikos 82:407–410.

Wilson, C. W., R. E. Masters, and G. A. Bukenhofer. 1995. Breeding bird response to pine-grassland community restoration for red-cockaded woodpeckers. J. Wildl. Manage. 59:56–67.

Wilson, E. O. 1987. The little things that run the world (the importance of conservation of invertebrates). Conservation Biology 1:344: 346.

Wolff, J. O., E. M. Schauber, and W. D. Edge. 1997. Effects of habitat loss and fragmentation on the behavior and demography of gray-tailed voles. Conservation Biology 11:945–956.

Yahner, R. H. 1995. Biodiversity conservation of butterflies and skippers in forested landscapes of Pennsylvania. Final Report. DCNR - Wild Resources Conservation Fund. 61.

Yahner, R. H. 1996. Biodiversity and conservation of butterflies and skippers in agricultural landscapes of Pennsylvania. Final Report. DCNR - Wild Resources Conservation Fund. 70.

Yahner, R. H. 1997. Butterfly and skipper communities in a managed forested landscape. Northeast Wildlife.

Yahner, R. H. 1998. Butterfly and Skipper use of nectar sources in forested and agricultural landscapes in Pennsylvania. J. Pa. Acad. Sci. 71(3):104–108.

Yahner, R. H., and B. D. Ross. 1995. Distribution and success of wood thrush nests in a managed forest landscape. Trans. Northeast Sect. Wildl. Soc. 52:1–9.

Yahner, R. H., B. D. Ross, and J. E. Kubel. 2004. Comprehensive inventory of birds and mammals at Fort Necessity National Battlefield and Friendship Hill National Historic Site. Technical Report NPS/NERCHAL/NRTR-04/093. National Park Service. Philadelphia, PA.

Yahner, R. H., and C. G. Mahan. 1997. Effects of logging roads on depredation of artificial ground nests in a forested landscape. Wildlife Society Bulletin 25:158–162.

Yahner, R. H., D. S. Klute, G. S. Keller, and B. D. Ross. 2001. Comprehensive inventory program for birds at six Pennsylvania national parks. Technical Report NPS/PHSP/NRTR-01/085. National Park Service. Philadelphia, PA.

Yao, J., R. D. Holt, P. M. Rich, and W. S. Marshall. 1999. Woody plant colonization in an experimentally fragmented landscape. Ecography 22:715–728.

Appendix. Recommended Vital Signs For Terrestrial Ecosystems.

The overall purpose of monitoring is to protect park resources "unimpaired for the enjoyment of future generations." Natural resource monitoring provides a basis for understanding and identifying meaningful change in natural systems characterized by complexity, variability, and surprises, and data may help to determine what constitutes impairment and to identify the need to initiate or change management practices. Vitals signs are physical, chemical, and biological elements and processes of park ecosystems that are selected to represent the overall health or condition of park resources, known or hypothesized effects of stressors, or elements that have important human values (USDI NPS, no date). To guide the monitoring program and the vital sign selection process, we present a list of proposed vitals signs (prepared by Hicks et al. 2005).

Vital Sign (VS) Number – Vital Sign Name
VS01 – Ozone
VS02 – Wet and Dry Deposition
VS04 – Weather and Climate
VS05 – Phenology
VS11 – Soil Erosion/Compaction
VS18 – Invasive Plants, Animals, Diseases – Status and Trends
VS20 – Forest Plant Communities – Structure and Demography
VS23 – Lichens, Liverworts, Mosses, Bryophytes, and Other Non-Vascular Plants
VS32 – Breeding Bird Community
VS34 – Terrestrial Invertebrates
VS38 – White-tailed Deer
VS48 – Reptiles and Amphibians
VS54 – Visitor Usage
VS58 – Ecosystem Pattern and Process
VS59 – Primary Production/Biomass Production
VS61 – Nutrient Dynamics

Level 1 ▶ Air and Climate
    Level 2 ▶ Air Quality
        Level 3 ▶ Ozone (VS01)

Brief Description: "Air Chemistry – Ozone" refers to the presence and amount of ozone (O^3) present in the ambient atmosphere of the National Park Service lands in the Eastern Rivers and Mountains Network (ERMN), as well as trends in ozone concentration over time. In addition to the atmospheric levels of ozone, the vital sign includes the symptoms of ozone damage displayed by sensitive plant species. The amount of ozone in the atmosphere is a primary predisposing factor affecting ecosystem health, whereas the symptoms of ozone damage displayed by sensitive plant species can be viewed as an indicator of ecosystem health relative to ozone (Chappelka and Samulson 1998).

Significance/Justification: The northeast and mid-Atlantic regions of the United States are areas well known for elevated levels of atmospheric ozone resulting from the burning of fossil fuels in the densely populated region, as well as the circulation of prevailing southwesterly wind patterns from the heavily industrialized Ohio Valley. An elevated level of ozone, since it is a regional climatic phenomenon, has the potential to affect the entire Eastern Mountains and Rivers Network, and could, therefore, have sweeping impacts over the whole system. Since ozone damage is manifested as foliar necrosis, its primary impact is on the plant's ability to carry out photosynthesis and to perform necessary physiological processes such as transpiration and mineral uptake. Therefore, plants with acute ozone damage are unable to efficiently use resources such as light, water, and mineral nutrients. For sensitive species, ozone damage will affect their health and fecundity, leading to a reduction in competitive ability. Loss of sensitive species may result in the loss of critical habitat and potential reduction in species diversity. Species that are sensitive to ozone damage provide an early warning system for ozone impacts, since they will show symptoms before other species do. This will permit the National Park Service to take action before the problem begins to directly affect non-sensitive organisms.

Proposed Metrics: For atmospheric ozone levels, the standard units of concentration (parts per million, etc.) should be used, so as to be consistent with on-going federal monitoring programs. For plant ozone damage the symptoms are somewhat subjective, but categories used by the USDA Forest Service and other federal agencies for monitoring sensitive species should be used (Skelly, et al. 1987).

Prospective Method(s) and Frequency of Measurement: Tonnie Maniero of the National Park Service Air Resources Division indicated (Draft report for Long-Term Ecological Monitoring, Phase 1) that all ERMN parks, except the Upper Delaware, have ozone monitors in place within 35 km (22mi). The Environmental Protection Agency (EPA), National Atmospheric Deposition Program (NADP) has maintained a network of monitoring stations for ozone over the past several years. These data serve as a benchmark for atmospheric ozone levels as well as a source of on-going data for future levels. The NADP data should serve as the primary source for the NPS in ozone monitoring, and has the added benefit of incurring no cost for measurement. Because the NADP system was not developed to specifically address the ozone levels in the ERMN, additional on-site monitoring stations may be advisable, as suggested by Maniero. Such automated stations can provide a continuous record of on-site atmospheric ozone levels. This can be very helpful in linking ozone levels to detected amounts of ozone damage. ERMN will need to develop a monitoring program for ozone-sensitive plant species in the individual parks. The NPS, ARD has determined that a "moderate to high risk of ozone injury to sensitive vegetation" exists in all ERMN parks. The USDA Forest Service, through the Forest Health Monitoring Program, document ozone damage to trees, but the intensity of such documentation and the location of monitoring points may not correspond to the needs of the ERMN. Furthermore, using on-site atmospheric monitoring stations, coupled with frequent symptom monitoring, can enable the detection of damage that may result from specific ozone "pulse" events. Smith et al. (2003) describe results from a national ozone biomonitoring program that should be valuable the ERMN.

Limitations of Data and Monitoring: A major limitation to this entire issue is the fact that the sources of ozone pollution are not directly controllable by the NPS, thus restoration of lost or damaged ecosystems may be difficult or impossible, especially if ozone levels continue to rise.

Key References:

Bardo, D. N., A. H. Chappelka, G. L. Somers, M. S. Miller-Goodman, and K. Stolte. 1998. Diversity of an early successional plant community as influenced by ozone. New Phytologist 138: 653-662.

Chappelka, A. H. and L. J. Samuelson. 1998. Ambient ozone effects on forest trees of the eastern United States: a review. New Phytologist 139:91-108.

Coulston, J. W., G. C. Smith, and W. D. Smith. 2003. Regional assessment of ozone sensitive tree species using bioindicator plants. Environmental Monitoring and Assessment, 83: 113-127.

Davison, A. W., and J. D. Barnes. 1998. Effects of ozone on wild plants. New Phytologist 139: 135-151.

Edwards, P., C. Huber, and F. Wood. 2004. Ozone exposure and implications for vegetation in rural areas of the central Appalachian Mountains, U.S.A. Environmental Monitoring and Assessment 98: 157-174.

Neufeld, H. S., E. H. Lee, J. R. Renfro, W. D. Hacker, and B. Yu. 1995. Sensitivity of seedlings of black cherry (*Prunus serotina* Ehrh.) to ozone in Great Smoky Mountains National Park.

Ollinger, S. V., J. D. Aber, and P. B. Reich. 1997. Simulating ozone effects on forest productivity: interactions among leaf-, canopy-, and stand level processes. Ecological Applications 7(4): 1237-1251.

Samuelson, L. J. and J. M. Kelly. 1997. Ozone uptake in *Prunus serotina*, *Acer rubrum*, and *Quercus rubra* forest trees of different sizes. New Phytologist 136: 255-264.

Skelly, J. M., D. D. Davis, W. Merrill, E. A. Cameron, H. D. Brown, D. B. Drummond, and L. S. Dochinger (eds.). 1987. Diagnosing injury to eastern forest trees: a manual for identifying damage caused by air pollution, pathogens, insects, and abiotic stresses.

National Acid Precipitation Assessment Program, Forest Response Program, Vegetation Survey Research Cooperative. University Park, PA: Agricultural Information Services, College of Agriculture, Department of Plant Pathology, Pennsylvania State University. 122p. http://www.fs.fed.us/r8/foresthealth/pubs/ozone/r8-pr25/ozoneh2.htm#top

Smith, G., J. Coulston, E. Jespen, and T. Prichard. 2003. A national ozone biomonitoring program- results from field surveys of ozone sensitive plants in northeastern forests (1994-2000). Environmental Monitoring and Assessment 87: 271-291.

Related Environmental Issues and Linked Vital Signs: Atmospheric ozone directly affects a number of ecosystem attributes, especially related to sensitive plant (T&E) species, biodiversity, etc. Indirect effects may be far-reaching and could include impacts such an enabling invasive species, loss of focal species or communities, impacts on lichens and fungi, effects on terrestrial invertebrates when key habitat is altered, etc (Edwards Huber and Wood 2004).

Overall Assessment: Atmospheric ozone can have significant impacts, both direct and indirect, on a number of ecosystem processes. Although much data currently exist on atmospheric ozone levels, it is not site-specific for ERMN parks. Furthermore, monitoring the presence of ozone-damage symptoms on sensitive vegetation would provide an early warning system for potential damage to less sensitive species and would allow for linkages to be developed between atmospheric ozone levels and the appearance of foliar damage. Unfortunately, atmospheric ozone levels are a regional phenomenon, generated from anthropogenic sources, which are difficult to control. Therefore, restoration of ozone-damaged ecosystems may be difficult or impossible. However, ozone monitoring and damage assessment should be relatively inexpensive to the NPS.

Level 1 ▶ Air and Climate
   Level 2 ▶ Air Quality
      Level 3 ▶ Wet and Dry Deposition (VS02)

Brief Description: "Wet and Dry Deposition; Contaminants" refers to a variety of aerosols (both particulate and chemical) that reside in the ambient atmosphere and are deposited on the National Park Service lands in the Eastern Rivers and Mountains Network (ERMN), as well as trends in their concentration over time. These materials may enter the atmosphere via point sources, such as smokestack emissions, or from agricultural or urban pesticide application, as well as from vehicular emissions, or salt spray from highways (Driscoll et al 2001). These pollutants/contaminants can affect the components of the terrestrial ecosystem in a variety of ways, including acidification (acidic deposition), nitrogen saturation, heavy metal toxicity, pesticide toxicity, visual impairment, etc (DeHays et al. 1999). For the most part, atmospheric pollutants are primary predisposing and inciting factors affecting ecosystem health.

Significance/Justification: All of the ERMN sites occur within or near areas of the northeast and mid-Atlantic regions of the United States that have a substantial rural/urban/agricultural interface as well as a significant influence from industrialization and power generation. Vehicular burning of fossil fuels in the densely populated region also contributes much to the atmospheric pollution load. These pollutants have potentially sweeping effects on the entire ERMN (Lovett 1994). Wet/dry depositional effects are manifested in a variety of ways, depending on the pollutant. Direct effects include foliar necrosis and dieback in plants. In other cases, pollutants may be directly toxic to plants, animals, or microorganisms. However, indirect effects that result, for example, from soil acidification and its effect on mineral cycling may be more significant in the long term. Atmospheric pollutants and contaminants potentially affect resources such as water and mineral nutrients. The long-term effects, such as altered litter decomposition, micro-flora and fauna, and altered nutrient cycling pose major threats to the health, fecundity, and sustainability of the ecosystems, and lead to an overall loss of species diversity.

Proposed Metrics: For atmospheric levels of wet/dry deposition, standard metrics that are consistent with Environmental Protection Agency (EPA) monitoring data should be used. For example, pH, parts per million, etc., are standard metrics used to quantify levels of substances in the atmosphere (Fox, Bernado and Hood 1987). For amounts of these substances being deposited to the landscape, standard collectors are used for sampling wet or dry deposition, and the amounts are usually expressed as a weight deposited per unit area over time (e.g. kg/ha/yr).

Prospective Method(s) and Frequency of Measurement: Tonnie Maniero, NPS, ARD, regarding wet/dry deposition, indicates that "the ERMN parks in Pennsylvania all have MDN monitors within 60 km (37 mi); none of the West Virginia parks have representative wet mercury deposition monitoring," and "with the exception of Upper Delaware S&RR, particulate matter is monitored within 35 km (22 mi) of all ERMN parks." Coverage of ERMN parks appears to be adequate for wet/dry deposition, for the most part. Where needed, additional stations can be installed on-site. As Maniero suggests, installation of automated digital cameras may be useful in vista areas where haze or pollutants threaten visibility. The Environmental Protection Agency maintains a network of monitoring stations for pollutants and deposition. These data can serve as a benchmark for atmospheric deposition levels as well as a source of on-going data for future levels.

Limitations of Data and Monitoring: Atmospheric pollution is often a problem of regional, even global proportions, therefore, it may be difficult or impossible to mitigate. Some situations may be more controllable than others, for example, dust coming from a local quarry or pesticide spray drift from a local farm may be relatively easy to address, whereas pollutants from vehicular emissions are impossible to control in the short term. The movement of wind and occurrence of unpredictable events such as air inversions makes monitoring of pollutants tricky (Weathers, Cadenasso and Pickett 2001).

Key References:

Asman, W. A. H., M. A. Sutton, and Schjorring. 1998. Ammonia: emission, atmospheric transport and deposition. New Phytologist 139: 27-48.

Cappellato, R., N. E. Peters, and T. P. Meyers. 1998. Above-ground sulfur cycling in adjacent coniferous and deciduous forests and watershed sulfur retention in the Georgia Piedmont, U.S.A. Water, Air, and Soil Pollution 103: 151-171.

DeHaynes, D. H., P. G. Schaberg, G. J. Hawley, and R. Stimbeck. 1999. Acid rain impacts calcium nutrition and forest health. BioScience 49: 789-800.

Driscoll, C. T., G .B. Lawrence, A. J. Bulger, T. J. Butler, C. S. Cronan, C. Eager, K. F. Lambert, G. E. Likens, J. L. Stoddard, and K. C. Weathers. 2001. Acidic deposition in the northeastern United States: sources and inputs, ecosystem effects, and management strategies. BioScience 51(3): 180-198.

Driscoll, C. T., K. M. Driscoll, M. J. Mitchell, and J. R. Dudley. 2003. Effects of acidic deposition o forest and aquatic ecosystems in New York State. Environmental Pollution 123: 327-336.

Fenn, M. E., R. Hauber, G. S. Tonnesen, J. S. Baron, S. Grossman-Clarke, D. Hope, D. A. Jaffe, S. Copeland, L. Geiser, H. M. Rueth, and J. O. Sickman. 2003. Nitrogen emissions, deposition, and monitoring in the western United States. BioScience, 53(4): 1-13.

Fox, D. G., J. C. Bernabo, and B. Hood. 1987. Guidelines for measuring the physical, chemical and biological condition of wilderness ecosystems. USDA Forest Service, Gen. Tech. Rep. Rm-146. p.48.

Garner, J. H. B., T. Pagano, and E. B. Cowling. 1989. Evaluation of the role of ozone, acid deposition, and other airborne pollutants in the forests of eastern North America. USDA Forest Service, SE-59. pp.189.

Johnson, D. W., and I. J. Fernandez. 1992. Soil Mediated Effects of Atmospheric Deposition on Eastern U.S. Spruce-Fir Forests. In C. Eager, M.B. Adams, eds., Ecology and Decline of Red Spruce in the Eastern United States. New York: Springer-Verlag.

Leith, I. D., M. B. Murray, L. J. Sheppard, J. N. Cape, J. D. Deans, R. I. Smith, and D. Fowler, 1989. Visible foliar injury of red spruce seedlings subjected to simulated acid mist. New Phytologist 113(3):313-320.

Lovett, G. M. 1994. Atmospheric deposition of nutrients and pollutants in North America: an ecological perspective. Ecological Applications 4(4):629-650.

McLaughlin, S. B., C. P. Anderson, P. J. Hanson, M. G. Tjoelker, and K. Roy. 1991. Increased dark respiration and calcium deficiency of red spruce in relation to acid deposition at high-elevation southern Appalachian Mountain sites. Can. J. For. Res. 21:1234-1244.

Shortle, W. C., K. T. Smith, R. Mincocha, G. B. Lawrence, and M. B. David. 1997. Acid deposition, cation mobilization, and stress in healthy red spruce trees. J. Environ. Qual. 26:871-876.

McLaughlin, D. 1998. A decade of forest tree monitoring in Canada: evidence of air pollution effects. Environmental Review 6(3-4):151-171.

Potter, C. S., H. L. Ragsdale, and W. T Swank. 1991. Atmospheric deposition and foliar leaching in a regenerating southern Appalachian forest canopy. Journal of Ecology 79:97-115.

Vann, D. R., A. H. Johnson, and B. B. Casper. 1994. Effects of elevated temperatures on carbon dioxide exchange in *Picea rubens*. Tree Physiology 14:1339-1349.

Weathers, K. C., M. L. Cadenasso, and S. T. A. Pickett. 2001. Forest edges as nutrient and pollutant concentrators: potential synergisms between fragmentation, forest canopies, and the atmosphere. Conservation Biology 15(6):1506-1514.

Related Environmental Issues and Linked Vital Signs: Atmospheric pollutants directly affect a number of ecosystem processes. In particular, soils can absorb and accumulate pollutants, altering nutrient cycling. Acidified soils have lower base saturation, and therefore, lower fertility, resulting in reduced bio-productivity. Runoff, throughfall, and direct input to streams and lakes can result in impacts to aquatic systems as well as terrestrial systems which can lead to loss of sensitive species.

Overall Assessment: Atmospheric pollutants, including acid deposition, SO_4, NO_3, particulates, heavy metals, etc. are prevalent in the EMRN region and can affect numerous ecosystem processes, including nutrient cycling, litter dynamics, and regeneration. Indirect effects of pollutants may be the enabling of invasive species and the loss of T&E species due to habitat alteration or direct toxicity. Amphibian species appear to be especially sensitive to water-borne pollutants. Because of the extensive baseline of data already in existence, the deployment of a monitoring system for the ERMN parks should be relatively inexpensive, but due to the regional nature of pollutants and the anthropogenic origin of many of them, mitigation and reclamation of damaged ecosystems will be difficult.

Brief Description: Weather and Climate are factors that have a direct effect on the health and competitive ability of long-lived perennial organisms like trees. Plants of a given species possess the genetic potential to exist within a particular range of temperature and moisture conditions, known as "cardinal limits" (Hicks, 1998). Furthermore, species are most competitive at certain conditions that are near the "ecological optimum" for their physiological processes. One of the most critical and controversial issues in the scientific community today is the prospect of global climate change, specifically, global warming. For example, Overpeck, Barlein and Webb (1991) propose that the global climate could warm by an average of 1.5-4.5 degrees C by the end of the twenty-first century. This, in turn, could lead to the migration of southern species to the north (Solomon and Kirilenko 1997) as well as local extirpation of species such as red spruce in the southern Appalachians (Adams et al. 1985). It is important to monitor the climatic changes in the ERMN and to link these changes to the health, productivity, and fecundity of sensitive and ecologically important species.

Significance/Justification: Weather and climate are predisposing factors affecting health and vigor of organisms and communities. When organisms are affected by climate change they are unable to efficiently use resources such as light, water, and mineral nutrients, and may become competitively disadvantaged relative to other species in the community. Climate change will affect the health and fecundity of organisms, leading to a reduction in competitive ability. Loss of sensitive species may result in the loss of critical habitat and potential reduction in species diversity. Because of the apparent global climate change that is predicted to continue for many decades, species that live at suboptimal fringes of their range are most at risk. The National Park Service is mandated to preserve unique biological resources in its parks; therefore, it is imperative that communities and organisms that are sensitive to global change in the parks be monitored carefully. Such species will serve as indicators of impact (De Groot, Ketner and Ovaa, 1995). Mahan (2004) provides lists of plants, vertebrates, and communities of special concern in the New River Gorge (NERI). Some of these species may be among the first to suffer from the effects of global climate change. Monitoring these species will permit the National Park Service to take action before non-sensitive organisms are affected.

Proposed Metrics: *Prospective Method(s) and Frequency of Measurement*: Metrics such as species importance values and indices to health and vigor of certain species deemed to be sensitive to climate change could be used to show impact. In addition, measures of species diversity can be used as potential indicators of climate-related problems. It is also important to track weather and climate in the parks, although the National Oceanic and Atmospheric Administration (NOAA) data may be adequate for this purpose without additional in-house tracking. Weather data that are important include daily, monthly, seasonal, and annual averages for maximum and minimum temperatures, and precipitation. In addition, growing season length is important.

Limitations of Data and Monitoring: One limitation to monitoring sensitive species is determining which ones are actually the best candidates as indicators. Secondly, if species are threatened or endangered, they will be difficult to find. In addition, taking measurements on T&E species may in itself cause stress to the species, and therefore may not be advisable. Finally, if indeed global climate change is occurring, it is not under the control of the NPS, thus restoration of lost or damaged ecosystems is probably not possible.

Key References:

Adams, H.S., Stephenson, S.L., Blasing, T.J., & Duvick, D.N. 1985. Growth-trend declines of spruce and fir in mid-Appalachian subalpine forests. Environmental and Experimental Botany 25(4): 315-325.

De Groot, R. S., P. Ketner, and A. H. Ovaa. 1995. Selection and use of bio-indicators to assess the possible effects of climate change in Europe. Journal of Biogeography 22: 935-943.

Hicks, R. R., Jr. 1998. Ecology and Management of Central Hardwood Forests. John Wiley and Sons, New York. 412 pp.

Iverson, L. R., M. W. Schwartz, and A. M. Prasad. 2004. Potential colonization of newly available tree-species habitat under climate change: an analysis for five eastern US species. Landscape Ecology 19: 787-799.

Johnson, A. H., E. R. Cook, and T. G. Siccama. 1988. Climate and red spruce growth and decline in the northern Appalachians. Proceedings of the National Academy of Sciences of the U.S.A. 85(15): 5369-5373.

Mahan, C. G. 2004. A Natural Resource Assessment for the New River Gorge National River. US Department of Interior, NPS Technical Report NPS/NER/NRTR—2004/002. 129 pp.

McLaughlin, S. and K. Percy. 1999. Forest health in North America: some perspectives on actual and potential roles of climate and air pollution. Water, Air, and Soil Pollution 116: 151-197.

Ojima, D. S., T. G. F. Kittel, T. Rosswall, and B. H. Walker. 1991. Critical issues for understanding global change effects on terrestrial ecosystems. Ecological Applications, 1(3): 316-325.

Overpeck, J. T., P. J. Barlein, and T. Webb, III. 1991. Potential magnitude of future vegetation change in eastern North America: comparisons with the past. Science 254(5032):692-695.

Parmesan, C., T. L. Root, and M. R. Willig. 2000. Impacts of extreme weather and climate on terrestrial biota. Bulletin of the Meteorological Society 81(3): 443-450.

Solomon, A. M., and A. P. Kirilenko. 1997. Climate change and terrestrial biomass: What if trees migrate? Global Ecology and Biogeography Letters 6(2): 139-148.

Related Environmental Issues and Linked Vital Signs: Weather and climate directly affect a number of other ecosystem attributes, especially related to sensitive and T&E species, biodiversity, etc. Because climate does not act in a vacuum, other vital signs such as levels of atmospheric pollution (VS1, VS2, VS3) may interact with climate to affect organisms. Indirect effects may occur such as the enabling of invasive species and loss of focal species or communities.

Overall Assessment: Climate plays a fundamental role in terrestrial ecosystems. Therefore, climatic changes have the potential to bring about substantial changes in the functional role of organisms, and thus, changes in communities. Climate change appears to be a global phenomenon caused by the accumulation of greenhouse gases in the atmosphere and is impossible to control at a local level. Therefore, restoration of climate-altered ecosystems may be difficult or impossible. However, good climatic data exist through the NOAA databases and is relatively inexpensive to the NPS. On the other hand, monitoring ecosystems to determine whether or not ecosystem changes are occurring in response to changing climate may be very difficult and expensive.

Level 1 ▶ Air and Climate
    Level 2 ▶ Weather and Climate
        Level 3 ▶ Phenology (VS5)

Brief Description: "Phenology" refers to the study of periodic events in biological organisms. For example, the timing of bud burst for dormant trees in the spring is a phonological event of interest. Phenology can be applied to any of a number of seasonal processes in plants, including cambial activation, root growth, starch-sugar conversion, leaf shed, onset of dormancy, etc. Behavior in animals (hibernation, migration, breeding) is also included under the study of phenology. Phenology can provide a bio-indicator for events that trigger plant or animal responses (temperature, solar flux, etc.), and therefore may serve as an indicator of global climate change, which, in turn, may alter ecosystem health (Badeck et al. 2004; Chuine, Cambon and Comtois 2000). In a Wisconsin study, spanning 61 years, it was apparent that phenological events have been increasing in earliness, and this apparently reflects climate change (Bradley et al. 1999).

Significance/Justification: The global climate is apparently dynamic, with prehistoric changes being linked to continental drift, shifting polar location, volcanic activity, meteor impacts, etc. In the modern world, anthropogenic activities have produced conditions that have been linked to global climate change, such as global warming resulting from the "greenhouse effect" caused by increased carbon dioxide emissions from burning fossil fuels. Phenology provides a convenient indicator of current seasonal climate, and taken over time, can provide a biological index for long-term climate change. Choices of phenological properties and species should focus on species that are sensitive to their environment (e.g. temperature) and those that represent different taxa (plant, animal), as well as different niches and guilds including overstory, understory, herbaceous, woody, amphibian, mammal, bird, etc.(Blaustein et al. 2001; Chuine and Beaubein 2001). Although phenology does not directly indicate ecological degradation, it may indicate events that will ultimately lead to degradation. Resources such as carbon dioxide, oxygen, heat, light, and water may all be involved or affected by the processes that are indicated by phenology. In the long term, phenological changes may indicate ecosystem changes that will affect species composition, diversity, bio-productivity, reproduction, regeneration, health, and fecundity.

Proposed Metrics: The metrics used for phenology are the dates of occurrence of events (e.g. bud break, cambial activation, flowering, reproductive behavior, hibernation, migration, etc.). In addition to these data, it will be important to compare the timing of these events with climatic data for the same periods. The use of models to integrate phenology with climatic data may be useful in predicting the response of organisms to global climate change, including shifts in geographic range (Post and Stenseth 1999).

Prospective Method(s) and Frequency of Measurement: In the eastern deciduous forests, typical of the ERMN parks, seasonal events often occur in the spring or fall. Mating seasons, initiation of growth, flowering, leaf fall, and bud break take place at these times; therefore, phenological observations should be timed to take advantage of these definitive seasonal events. A repeatable measure should be chosen, for example the point at which all leaves are fully expanded, when flowers are fully opened, or when pollen is being shed. These measurements should be replicated annually on the same species, being careful to use the same or similar microsites (e.g. north-facing slope at 300 m elevation).

Limitations of Data and Monitoring: One limitation of phenological data is the fact that different observers may interpret a particular point (such as fully expanded leaves) in different ways. Another problem is the fact that organisms may be responding to several environmental elements that are changing in different ways. For example, photoperiod is consistent from year to year, whereas rainfall and temperature may vary in different ways in different years, confounding the effect that one of these factors may have independent of the others. This is part of the rationale for maintaining long-tern phenological records on the same species.

Key References:

Al-Mufti, M. M., C. L. Sydes, S. B. Furness, and S. R. Band. 1977. A quantitative analysis of shoot phenology and dominance in herbaceous vegetation. Journal of Ecology 65(3): 759-791.

Badeck, F. W., A. Bondeau, K. Bottcher, D. Doktor, W. Lucht, J. Schaber, and S. Sitch. 2004. Research Review: Responses of spring phenology to climate change. New Phytologist 162: 295-309.

Blaustein, A. R., L. K. Belden, D. H. Olson, D. M. Green, T. L. Root, and J. M. Kiesecker. 2001. Amphibian breeding and climate change. Conservation Biology 15(6): 1804-1809.

Bradley, N. L., A. C. Leopold, J. Ross, and W. Huffaker. 1999. Phenological changes reflect climate change in Wisconsin. Proc. Natl. Acad. Sci. 96(17): 9701-9704.

Burke, M. K., and D. J. Raynal. 1994. Fine root growth phenology, production, and turnover in a northern hardwood forest ecosystem. Plant and Soil 162: 135-146.

Chuine, I. & G. Beaubien. 2001. Phenology is a major determinant of tree species range. Ecology Letters 4:500-510.

Chuine, I., G. Cambon, and P. Comtois. 2000. Scaling phenology from the local to the regional level: advances from species-specific phenological models.

Chuine, I., and P. Cour. 1999. Climatic determinants of budburst seasonality in four temperate-zone tree species. New Phytologist 143: 339-349.

Gibbs, J. P., and A. R. Breisch. 2001. Climate warming and calling phenology of frogs near Ithaca, New York, 1900-1999. Conservation Biology 15(4):1175-1178.

Langvatn, R., S. D. Albon, T. Burkey, and T. H. Clutton-Brock. 1996. Climate, plant phenology and variation in age of first reproduction in a temperate herbivore. Journal of Animal Ecology 65(5): 653-670.

Post, E., and N. C. Stenseth. 1999. Climatic variability, plant phenology, and northern ungulates. Ecology 80(4): 1322-1339.

Walther, G-R., E. Post, P. Convey, A. Menzel, C. Parmesan, T. J. C. Beebee, J-M. Fromentin, O. Hoegh-Guldberg, and F. Bairlein. 2002. Ecological responses to recent climate change. Nature 416: 389-395.

White, M. A., P. E. Thornton, and S. W. Running. 1997. A continental phenology model for monitoring vegetation responses to inter annual climatic variability. Global Biochemical cycles 11(2): 217-234.

Related Environmental Issues and Linked Vital Signs: Phenology as an indicator is particularly suited to monitor global climate changes. Therefore, it is especially linked with weather and climate. To the extent that phenology indicates changes in climate, phenological changes for one or a few species may indicate broader ecosystem changes as well. These changes may alter interspecific competition and biodiversity (VS20).

Overall Assessment: Phenology is an indicator of differing environmental conditions, especially weather-related conditions that, over time, can amount to climate change. Long-term monitoring of certain phenological events for particular species can establish a baseline to determine if climate change is occurring, and will aid managers in developing strategies to preserve at-risk populations. Phenological studies require little specialized equipment and will mostly require observers to collect the field data and a process for data management. Therefore, phenological observations should be relatively inexpensive, but should yield useful results.

Brief Description: "Soil Erosion/Compaction" refers to processes that occur in which residual soil is compacted and/or lost from a site, usually through the action of water. Compaction is the effect that takes place when soil is subjected to heavy or repeated pressure, thereby reducing its pore space and increasing its bulk density (Shestak and Busse 2005). Soil erosion literally takes the soil, and its included nutrients and water-holding capacity, away from a site, and in so doing, denies plants and animals of resources such as oxygen, mineral nutrients, and water. Compaction also reduces available oxygen and restricts root growth in the soil which, in turn, may result in de-vegetation of the compacted area, which is often followed by erosion (Deluca et al. 1998). These are two of the most destructive processes relating to soils, and soils form the basis for plant life in terrestrial communities. The USDA, Natural Resource Conservation Service (NRCS) and the Soil Science Society of America (SSSA) provide standard methods for assessing soil loss and compaction that can be applied to high use areas in the EMRN parks. Soil erosion/compaction can be a contributing factor to altered ecosystem health.

Significance/Justification: Soil forms the basis for terrestrial ecosystems. It is a complex mixture of organic and inorganic fractions and provides support as well as minerals, water, and oxygen to plants (Powers et al. 2004). Particularly in high-use areas of the ERMN parks, soils are at risk for compaction and erosion, especially in heavily traveled areas such as trails, overlooks, and historic sites (Deluca et al. 1998). Ironically, the very reason these sites have significance is because people find them interesting and unique. But overuse or poorly planned use may destroy the very resources that make the parks unique in the first place. Compacted soils often are difficult for plant roots to penetrate and have reduced aeration and poor water holding capacity. This may lead to the loss of mesofauna and vegetation (Battigelli et al. 2004), which, in turn, leads to erosion and soil loss. Over time compaction and erosion will degrade the site leading to reduced diversity, bio-productivity, regeneration, health, and fecundity of the plant community. This will adversely impact the fauna of the system as well. Once soil has eroded from a site it often appears as sediment in nearby streams, thus creating another environmental problem.

Proposed Metrics: The NRCS uses the Universal Soil Loss Equation to predict soil loss from eroded sites as weight of soil lost per unit area of land. For soil compaction, the standard measure is bulk density, expressed as weight per unit volume of soil.

Prospective Method(s) and Frequency of Measurement: Soil erosion can be measured by placing stakes in the soil and periodically measuring the exposed height of the stake to indicate the amount of soil lost. Erosion stakes should be strategically placed in high use areas such as paths and trails, picnic areas, overlooks, and historic sites. To serve as a control, stakes should also be placed in low-use areas as well. The erosion stakes should be measured at least three times each year, during the high-use season (usually summer into fall). In addition, soil bulk density measurements should be taken at the same high-use sites. There are several methods for bulk density measurement, including some that require removal of soil for weight and volume determination, and others that use a probe to determine the resistance of the soil to penetration. For the latter, the method is not well suited to soils with high rock content. Bulk densities should be taken at least once per season (preferably in the fall), and as with the erosion measurement, control sites should be included that are outside the high traffic areas.

Limitations of Data and Monitoring: As with any data that are acquired by sampling, the validity of the data is a function of the adequacy of the sampling system. Using a large number of samples is always better than a small sample. However, if the experimental unit is a single site at a park, the number of samples to adequately represent that site may be quite large, as opposed to the case where soil erosion/compaction data are intended to represent the whole park or the entire ERMN system. Decisions will have to be made by the managers as to which scenario they wish to monitor, and, ultimately, the limitation may be determined by how many samples they can afford to collect.

Key References:

Deluca, T. H., W.A. Patterson, IV, W. A. Freimund, and D. N. Cole. 1998. Influence of llamas, horses, and hikers on soil erosion from established recreation trails in western Montana, USA. Environmental Management, 22(2): 255-262.

Gomez, A., R. F. Powers, M. J. Singer, and W. R. Horwath. 2002. N uptake and N status in ponderosa pine as affected by soil compaction and forest floor removal. Plant and Soil, 242: 263-275.

Ponder, Jr., F. 2004. Ecological regions and soil conditions in the Hoosier-Shawnee Ecological Assessment Area. USDA, Forest Service. Gen. Tech. Rept. NC-244, 267 p.

Powers, R. F., F. G. Sanchez, D. A. Scott, and D. Page-Dumbroese. 2004. The North American long-term soil productivity experiment: coast-to-coast findings from the first decade. USDA Forest Service RMRS-P-34.

Related Environmental Issues and Linked Vital Signs: Soil productivity is directly related to soil erosion and compaction. The soil fauna and flora as well as nutrient cycling are affected by compaction and erosion. Bio-productivity and regeneration may also be affected. Certain T&E species could be directly affected by these conditions, and soil that is lost from a terrestrial site may end up as silt and sediment in a nearby aquatic system.

Overall Assessment: Soil is the primary medium for plant growth, providing support as well as oxygen, minerals, and water for plant growth. Compaction and erosion are most likely to occur in and around high-use areas of the ERMN parks, and a monitoring system to detect levels of erosion and compaction should focus on these sites. Depending on the chosen experimental unit (site, park, system), the sampling scheme may be rather elaborate and collecting and processing samples could be labor-intensive and time-consuming. If such is the case, proper soil compaction/erosion data could be expensive to collect and analyze. But, considering the damage that may be occurring due to over use or improper use, the investment may be worth it. Soil erosion/compaction is an issue that is within the direct control of park managers and preventative or remedial activities such as restricting access and rerouting or paving trails can have immediate benefits to the ecosystem.

Level 1 ► **Biological Integrity**
    Level 2 ► **Invasive Species**
        Level 3 ► **Invasive Plants, Animals, Diseases – Status and Trends (VS18)**

Brief Description: "Invasive Plants, Animals, Diseases – Status and Trends" is a very broad subject, including 1) invasive plants and animals whose primary effect is displacement of native species and 2) species of exotic insects, animals, or pathogens that attack and cause injury or death to native species. Examples of the former are tree-of-heaven, whorled loosestrife, and garlic mustard, whereas examples of the latter include nutria, beech bark disease, gypsy moth, chestnut blight, and hemlock wooly adelgid. An abundance of invasive plants and animals is often associated with disturbed or degraded ecosystems (Burke and Carino 2000); therefore, their presence serves as an indicator of ecosystem health. On the other hand, invasive species, including insect and disease pests, can dramatically alter an ecosystem (serving as an inciting factor for ecosystem decline), thus directly affecting processes such as succession, regeneration, and mineral cycling. Furthermore, the altered ecosystem state may result in a system that is unhealthy, has lower diversity, and has reduced fecundity of native species. Invasive species, including insects and diseases, have resulted in dramatic historic changes to numerous ecosystems in North America, including the ERMN area. Examples include chestnut blight, which has all but eliminated a species that once defined much of the Mid-Atlantic region, and gypsy moth, which has caused extreme damage and major ecosystem changes throughout the region. The recent invasion of the hemlock wooly adelgid indicates that the potential risk from invasive organisms remains significant.

Significance/Justification: Native plants and animals that make up a particular ecosystem have co-evolved over millions of years; therefore, native ecosystems have developed a state of dynamic equilibrium. The introduction of nonnative species into a system can upset this balance. Because of the globalization of human activities, including travel, shipping, and deliberate species introduction for food and agricultural purposes, many species have been moved from their native ranges and have been introduced to exotic environments around the world. In most cases, these species have been unsuccessful or have blended into the local environment with minor impacts. But for some species, their introduction has led to their becoming "invasive." This term refers to the condition that exists when a nonnative plant or animal becomes highly aggressive in its new environment and causes habitat destruction, replacement of native species, or results in damaging outbreaks. National parks are especially vulnerable to species invasion because of the large number of visitors who enter the parks and serve as potential vectors of invasive organisms. At the forest community level resources such as light, mineral nutrients, and water are affected when invasive species either displace or attack and kill native species. Invasive organisms can bring about alterations in species composition, bio-productivity, regeneration, and nutrient cycling, changing the diversity, vigor, and fecundity of the ecosystem. The direct effects of an invasion include species displacement, infestation, and mortality of host species, but indirect effects such as shifts in species composition, altered nutrient cycling, and modified temperature and light regimes often have more profound impacts than the direct effects (Kizinski et al. 2002). The introduction of organisms has resulted in greater and more lasting ecosystem damage than virtually anything brought about by humans in recent history (Pimentel et al. 2000).

Proposed Metrics: In situations where an invading organism has not yet fully colonized a suitable habitat, the metric chosen to describe the colonization is usually the rate of advancement of the infestation or killing front. In the case where a non-invasive form of an organism precedes the invasive or reproductive stage (such as is the case when male gypsy moths precede the flightless female into an non-infested area), the presence and numbers of male moths can serve as an indication of the potential for invasion by reproductive populations. In areas where infestation or invasion has already occurred, the numbers of invading organisms per unit area or the proportion of the suitable habitat that has been colonized can be a valuable metric. Finally, the presence and impact of an insect or disease is often measured by the number or proportion of hosts that are colonized or killed. This would be particularly useful where the populations of invading organisms are very large and difficult to measure and the value of the host is great, for example with beech bark disease and hemlock wooly adelgid (Morin et al. 2005).

Prospective Method(s) and Frequency of Measurement: Surveys of damaging insects and diseases of forest ecosystems are conducted by federal agencies such as the USDA Forest Service as well as by state agencies such as the West Virginia Department of Agriculture, Plant Industries Division. For newly introduced organisms that are potentially damaging, records and surveys are conducted by the USDA, Animal and Plant Health Inspection Service. Before any in-house programs are undertaken by the ERMN, this information should be investigated to determine whether or not it meets the needs of the NPS. Furthermore, hazard rating systems that have been developed, especially in the case of insects and diseases, may be useful in determining whether or not a particular park is likely to have a problem with an invading organism. Once it is determined that a need exists for additional on-site surveys for an invading organism, the appropriate sampling scheme should be developed and tailored to the specific situation. With a problem as broad and diverse as invasive plants, animals, insects and diseases, surveys will need to be developed that are capable of detecting damaging populations and fulfilling the needs of the ERMN.

Limitations of Data and Monitoring: Perhaps the greatest limitation of monitoring for invasive organisms is the sheer magnitude of the task. The ERMN parks occupy extensive areas of land and are situated in areas with large and remote forested components. Organisms can quickly spread from non-system lands onto parks. Invasive organisms can persist below detection levels and rapidly explode into outbreaks when favorable conditions occur. Data collected only on NPS lands will be of limited value in predicting the ambient population levels and therefore may not be useful in preventing spread of organisms from adjacent ownerships. It is incumbent upon the NPS to choose carefully which organisms to focus on, concentrating on those most likely to do significant damage to the parks, and to utilize data collected by other agencies, whenever possible.

Key References:

Blossey, B. 1999. Before, during and after: the need for long-term monitoring in invasive plant species management. Biological Invasions, 1: 301-311.

Burke, M. J. W., and J. P. Grime. 1996. An experimental study of plant community invasibility. Ecology, 77(3): 776-790.

Daehler, C. C. and D. A. Carino. 2000. Predicting invasive plants: prospects for a general screening system based on current regional models. Biological Invasions 2: 93-102.

Davis, M. A., J. P. Grime, and K. Thompson. 2000. Fluctuating resources in plant communities: a general theory of invasibility. Journal of Ecology 88: 528-534.

Gammon, D. E. and B. A. Maurer. 2002. Evidence for non-uniform dispersal in the biological invasions of two naturalized North American bird species. Global Ecology & Biogeography 11: 155-161.

Hicks, R. R., Jr., and D. A. Mudrick. 1993. Forest health: a status report for West Virginia. WV Dept. of Agriculture. P. 68.

Howard, T. G., J. Gurevitch, L. Hyatt, M. Carreiro, and M. Lerdau. 2004. Forest invasibility in communities in southeastern New York. Biological Invasions 6: 393-410.

Kizlinski, M. L., D. A. Orwig, R. C. Cobb, and D. R. Foster. 2002. Direct and indirect ecosystem consequences of an invasive pest on forests dominated by eastern hemlock. Journal of Biogeography 29(10-11): 1489.

Manion, P. D. 1981. Tree Disease Concepts. Prentice-Hall, Inc. Englewood Cliffs, NJ. 339 pp.

McClure, M. S., and C. A. S.-J. Cheah. 1999. Reshaping the ecology of invading populations of hemlock woolly adelgid, *Adelges tsugae* (Homoptera: Adelgidae), in eastern North America. Biological Invasions 1: 247-254.

Morin, R. S., A. M. Liebhold, E. R. Luzader, A. J. Lister, K. W. Gottschalk, and D. B. Twardus. 2005. Mapping host-species abundance of three major exotic forest pests. USDA Forest Service Research Paper. NE-726. P. 15.

Orwig, D. A., and D. R. Foster. 1998. Forest response to the introduced Hemlock Woolly Adelgid in southern New England, USA. Journal of the Torrey Botanical Society 125(1):60-73.

Pimentel, D., L. Lach, R. Zuniga, and D. Morrison. 2000. Environmental and economic costs of nonindigenous species in the United States. BioScience 50(1):53-65.

USDA Forest Service. 1993. Northeastern Area Forest Health Report. USDS Forest Service. NA-TP-03-93.

With, K. A. 2002. The landscape ecology of invasive spread. Conservation Biology 16(5):1192-1203.

Related Environmental Issues and Linked Vital Signs: Species invasion could be linked with air and climate, such that an altered climatic regime may predispose a site to being invaded. Invasive species may displace plants and/or animals from unique natural communities, and this is especially true for T&E species, which may be living close to the limits of their existence in the absence of aggressive competitors.

Overall Assessment: Invasive plants, animals, diseases – status and trends is a very broad topic, and includes both exotic invasive species that displace natural species or communities as well as insects and diseases that injure or kill native species. These agents are, however, some of the most damaging of those affecting current terrestrial ecosystems. Their spread is directly related to human activities, either deliberate, accidental, or unintentional. This makes them all the more significant in National Parks where human visitation rate is high. Surveys of invasive organisms and damaging insects and diseases are routinely conducted by several federal and state agencies within the ERMN, and data from these surveys is public domain, therefore, inexpensive or free to acquire (USDA, Forest Service 1993). But for certain key species, the NPS may wish to develop their own on-site survey data. The decisions regarding which species and how to sample for them should be weighed carefully, since valid surveys may be difficult, expensive, and time consuming.

Brief Description: "Forest Plant Communities – Structure and Demography" deals with plants occupying all strata within stands (canopy, mid-story, understory) and it is specific to the stages of succession and stand dynamics (regeneration, stem exclusion, understory reinitiation, old-growth) that characterize the various communities within the ERMN parks. Owing to the successional stage, disturbance history, and the site it occupies, there are certain parameters within which a community can be described as healthy. By measuring the structural and demographic features of a given community an assessment can be made as to whether or not the ecosystem's parameters fall within expected norms. If not, it should raise concerns on the part of park managers to determine why the community is in an unhealthy state and would trigger actions to remediate and restore the community to a healthy state. Thus, structure and demography serve as indicators of ecosystem health.

Significance/Justification: Determining ecosystem health, as with any diagnostic activity, requires knowledge about key processes. This knowledge serves a function similar to that of diagnostic testing in medical science. Ecologists utilize standard descriptors to characterize the structure and demography of ecosystems or communities depending on the stages of development of the ecosystem, such as regeneration, stem exclusion, understory reinitiation, and old-growth. At each stage it is important to document the parameters that describe the health of the ecosystem so that managers can determine which communities require attention so they can assign priorities for remedial work. Ecosystem health affects processes such as bio-productivity, regeneration, succession, and nutrient cycling.

Proposed Metrics: The standard measures of demography include classification of forest communities into stages of development (regeneration, stem exclusion, understory reinitiation, old growth). These stages are somewhat subjective, therefore, classification is interpretive. Measures of structure include stratification of crowns into dominant, codominant, intermediate, and overtopped classes. Measures of stocking include basal stocking (e.g. square meters per hectare), number of trees per unit area, and percent stocking relative to some fully stocked norm. Measures such as importance values are also used to characterize the structure of a forest community. Understories are often described in terms of area coverage by non-woody species and numbers per unit area for woody species (trees, shrubs, etc.). Tree seedlings in the understory are usually categorized by shade tolerance and size classes, both of which have a strong bearing on their future success. Species diversity as also a measure of the state of a community and standard measures of diversity include species richness, Shannon-Weiner H', and Simpson's Index.

Prospective Method(s) and Frequency of Measurement: An "ecological inventory" will be required to acquire data needed to assess the demographics and structure of ecosystems. These inventories should involve permanent sample plots and these should be revisited at regular intervals (e.g. annually). Sampling should be stratified by the types of ecosystems (stages of development, etc.) present in each park. The size and needed number of such plots will depend on the size, density, and variability of the organisms and/or populations being sampled, as well as the degree of accuracy desired. Smaller plots, in the range of 3–4 m^2 (10–13 ft^2), that may be useful for sampling understory and regeneration, will not be suitable for overstory sampling. Hence, much larger plots would be necessary to characterize the tree strata. Data collected in an ecological inventory should be those that can be used to compute the standard ecological parameters, including tree species, dbh, total height, assessment of vigor, site conditions, understory coverage, and species and density of regeneration. Healthy ecosystems are dynamic, therefore, changes are to be expected. However, when the rate and nature of change deviates from the expected norm it may be a cause for concern to park managers. For example, when a certain species that was abundant in previous inventories begins to drop out at a more rapid rate than expected, or when regeneration is failing to ascend beyond the seedling stage, it would be a cause for concern. Sources of data such as the USDA Forest Service, Forest Inventory and Analysis (FIA), can provide a background to compare with ecological inventory data, but since the FIA data do not directly address many ecological issues, the ERMN will most likely find it necessary to establish their own data base.

Limitations of Data and Monitoring: In order to establish a reliable network of permanent samples it will require considerable effort and expense. Furthermore, in order for the data to have any real utility, it will require long-term commitment to the remeasurement of plots and the analysis and interpretation of data.

Key References:

Carignan, V., and M. Villard. 2002. Selecting indicator species to monitor ecological integrity: a review. Environmental Monitoring and Assessment, 78: 45-61.

Chase, M. K., W. B. Kristan, III, A. J. Lynam, M. V. Price, and J. T. Rotenberry. 2000. Single species as indicators of species richness and composition in California coastal sage scrub birds and small mammals. Conservation Biology 14(2): 474-487.

Dufrene, M., and P. Legendre. 1997. Species assemblages and indicator species: the need for a flexible asymmetrical approach. Ecological Monographs 67(3): 345-366.

Hicks, R. R., Jr., and J. L. Holt. 1999. Comparison of ecological characteristics of three remnant old-growth woodlots in Belmont County, Ohio. *In* Proc. 12th Cent. Hardwood Forest Conference. Lexington, KY.

Kintsch, J. A., and D. L. Urban. 2002. Focal species, community representation, and physical proxies as conservation strategies: a case study in the Amphibolite Mountains, North Carolina, U.S.A. Conservation Biology 16(4):936-947.

Lambeck, R. J. 1997. Focal species: a multi-species umbrella for nature conservation. Conservation Biology, 11(4):849-856.

Landres, P. B., J. Verner, and J. W. Thomas. 1988. Ecological uses of vertebrate indicator species: a critique. Conservation Biology 2(4):316-328.

Weaver, J. C. 1995. Indicator species and scale of observation. Conservation Biology 9(4):939-942.

Related Environmental Issues and Linked Vital Signs: The structure and demography of terrestrial communities is related to almost all the vital signs under the heading of "Biological Integrity" (VS18- VS50). Also, all the vital signs under the heading of "Ecosystem Pattern and Process" (VS57- VS61) are associated with plant community structure and demography. There are numerous inter-connections and feedback relationships among these biological resource groups. For example, forest structure and demography directly affects breeding bird communities, and birds also affect forests as vectors of seeds, insects, and fungal spores. Birds are also consumers of insects, and as such, they may be beneficial to infested plants.

Overall Assessment: Ecosystems respond to their environment, and plants communities are generally dictated by the environment within which they grow. Many species of plants are said to be "site specific" such as ginseng, which is often associated with the most productive sites, or mountain laurel which generally occurs on lower-quality sites. Plant populations also change their environment, and as the environment changes new species become more adapted, hence, the process of succession. As primary producers, plant communities supply energy for all trophic levels above them and are the key element in supplying niches for other species that inhabit the community. The structure of a plant community, apart from its energy relations, also contributes to habitat by supplying such things as nesting sites, escape cover, and vocalization sites for birds. Because of the importance of plant community structure and demography to the ecological health of ERMN parks these are attributes which should be closely monitored. Normal (successional) ecosystem changes are expected to occur, but when ecosystems are changing in ways that do not conform to expected norms for healthy ecosystems it is important for park managers to be aware of this, enabling them to respond appropriately.

Level 1 ▶ Biological Integrity
    Level 2 ▶ Focal Species or Communities
        Level 3 ▶ Lichens, Liverworts, Mosses, Bryophytes and other Non-Vascular Plants (VS23)

Brief Description: "Lichens, Liverworts, Mosses, Bryophytes, and Other Non-vascular Plants" are species that are typically found in forests of the ERMN. Because of their limited commercial value these species have been pretty much ignored by researchers in applied fields such as forestry. The exception is when such species are perceived to deter regeneration of commercial tree species. However, owing to the fact that several of these species are epiphytes, growing on trees or on bare rock surfaces, they are sensitive to the effects of atmospheric pollution, such as sulfates (Bates, Mcnee and Mcleod, 1996) or heavy metals (Insarov, Semenov and Insarova, 1999). These species may be useful indicators of ecosystem health. Declining abundance and diversity of non-vascular plants should raise concerns on the part of park managers regarding the health of the ecosystem and should initiate actions to remediate and restore the community to a healthy state.

Significance/Justification: Many non-vascular plants live as epiphytes, or in exposed locations such as cliffs, rocks, dead logs, etc. As such, they are exposed to extreme conditions, especially relating to moisture and temperature. They rely on nutrients dissolved in rainwater or deposited in particulate matter from the atmosphere. For this reason, such plants are vulnerable to changes in the chemistry of the atmosphere and precipitation. For example, in tropical cloud forests Gordon, Herrera and Hutchinson (1995) chose an epiphytic lichen as an indicator of the impact of atmospheric trace metals, and Vokou, Pirintsos and Loppi (1999) found a general impoverishment of lichen communities in forests of northern Greece, presumably due to atmospheric pollution. Non-vascular plants play a role in forest ecosystems by providing habitat for a variety of insects and small vertebrates.

Proposed Metrics: Little information is available regarding the non-vascular communities of the ERMN parks. At the NERI, Weeks, Nash and Nowland (1997) conducted the only known survey of non-vascular plants, and reported 14 species, mostly mosses. The best metrics for non-vascular species would be measures of density (relative area coverage) as well as measures of diversity such as species richness, the Shannon-Weiner H' and Simpson's Index.

Prospective Method(s) and Frequency of Measurement: An in-depth inventory of the current populations of non-vascular species should be conducted at each park. These inventories should involve permanent GPS-referenced sample locations and these should be revisited at regular intervals (e.g. 2- to 5-year intervals). Sampling should be stratified by the types of ecosystems (stages of development, cover type, etc.) present in each park. The method of sampling should reflect the organism being inventoried. For example, for mosses a fixed area plot might be the method of choice, using a relatively large plot (e.g. 0.4 ha), whereas sampling epiphytic lichens may be done on individual trees (stratified by species and size classes), or other structures, using the same trees/structure at each subsequent sampling period. For most non-vascular species the variable of interest will be the relative area coverage by species (e.g. m^2/ha). The number of plots/trees needed for a reliable sample will depend on the variability encountered when sampling the organisms, as well as the degree of accuracy desired. The initial inventory will serve as a baseline, and subsequent samples will be used to determine if the populations of non-vascular plants are changing with time. Since forests are constantly changing through processes such as succession and disturbance events, changes in non-vascular communities would be expected. However, if non-vascular plant communities appear to be changing at a rate that is inconsistent with natural processes, it may be a cause for concern.

Limitations of Data and Monitoring: In order to establish a reliable network of permanent samples it will require considerable effort and expense. Furthermore, in order for the data to have any real utility it will require long-term commitment to the remeasurement of plots and the analysis and interpretation of data.

Key References:

Bates, J.W., Mcnee, P.J., & Mcleod, A.R. 1996. Effects of sulphur dioxide and ozone on lichen colonization of conifers in the Liphook Forest Fumigation Project. New Phytologist, 132(4): 653-660.

Glenn, M., S. L. Webb, and M. S. Cole. 1998. Forest integrity at anthropogenic edges: air pollution disrupts bioindicators. Environmental Monitoring and Assessment 51:163-169.

Gordon, C. A., R. Herrera, and T. C. Hutchinson. 1995. The use of a common epiphytic lichen as a bioindicator of atmospheric inputs to two Venezuelan Cloud Forest. Journal of Tropical Ecology 11(1):1-26.

Insarov, G. E., S. M. Semenov, and R. D. Insarova. 1999. A system to monitor climate change with epilithic lichens. Environmental Monitoring and Assessment 55:279-298.

Vokou, D., S. A. Pirintsos, and S. Loppi. 1999. Lichens as bioindicators of temporal variations in air quality around Thessaloniki, northern Greece. Ecological Research 14:89-96.

Weaks, T. E.., D. Nash, and M. Nowland. 1997. Lichen and non-vascular flora of New River Gorge National River, West Virginia. Final Report. NERI, Glen Jean, WV.

Related Environmental Issues and Linked Vital Signs: Non-vascular plants, because of their dependence on trees and other structures for support, are very dependent on the type of overstory community present (VS20), which in turn is related to the presence and severity of agents of ecosystem change, such as insects and diseases (VS18), visitor usage (VS54), and white-tailed deer (VS38). Also, because of their vulnerability to weather and atmospheric conditions, non-vascular plants are especially sensitive to climate and pollutants (VS1, VS2, VS3, VS4).

Overall Assessment: Non-vascular plants are an area about which limited information is currently available, but they are potentially useful indicators of ecosystem health. An initial inventory of species (relative area of coverage and diversity) would serve as a baseline for subsequent samples. The changes observed, over time, may correlate with known changes in the environment or may trigger investigations to determine what is changing. Long-term stability of populations of non-vascular plants would be one indicator of ecosystem stability. Because little data on non-vascular species exist for the ERMN parks, an initial inventory will likely require a major commitment of personnel and funds.

Brief Description: The "Breeding Bird Community" refers to resident or neotropical migrant species of avifauna in the ERMN parks. Most of the species of importance in the ERMN system are forest-dwelling species, although some species that prefer open habitats may actually be relatively rare in the ERMN. Breeding birds are especially sensitive to habitat features such as canopy structure, nesting sites, food supplies, and escape cover (Conner and Dickson 1997). Some species of birds, such as woodpeckers, may serve as indicators of overall bird diversity (Mikusinski, Gromadzki and Chylarecki 2001). Birds have been shown to be useful indicators of ecosystem health, and this is especially true where ecosystems are heavily impacted (Bradford et al. 1998; O'Connell, Jackson and Brooks 2001). Declining abundance and diversity of sensitive bird species should be of concern to park managers since birds indicate overall ecosystem health and are a resource that is sought after and appreciated by many park visitors.

Significance/Justification: It is clear that populations of breeding birds are associated with their habitat, which may in turn reflect the health of the ecosystem. For example, in the Savannah River of South Carolina (SRS), Kilgo et al. (2000) found that bird species that preferred urban and agricultural habitats were more abundant off the SRS, while forest-interior species such as the cerulean warbler were more abundant within the relatively undisturbed SRS. One advantage of using breeding birds as indicators of ecosystem health is the fact that historical data exist regarding their populations. One example is the North American Breeding Bird Survey (Sauer et al. 2000); and more specific to the ERMN is a survey reported by Yahner et al. (2001) that was taken in six Pennsylvania National Parks, including the Allegheny Portage Railroad National Historic Site and the Johnstown Flood National Memorial. These surveys can serve as a baseline for assessing future trends on breeding bird populations. Finally, bird populations are important assets of National Parks, and to the extent that the ERMN parks contain unique habitat, they will also contain populations of birds that visitors will be drawn to.

Proposed Metrics: Metrics such as relative abundance of particular species (Bradford et al. 1998) or guilds (Jones et el. 2000), as well as overall species richness for species or guilds, appear to be the most common means of assessing bird populations. These measurements are meaningful when tracked over time.

Prospective Method(s) and Frequency of Measurement: Bird presence and density are usually established by counts and/or reports from trained observers. These take the form of singing male surveys, counts of birds in migrating flocks, nesting surveys, bird banding/recovery studies, and mist netting, or combinations of these. The particular method selected depends on the species to be inventoried. These inventories should be compared to historic baselines and previous inventories for the same areas. Therefore, the same areas should be sampled annually using the same methods (Beard, Scott and Adomson 1999). Sampling should be stratified proportional to the types of ecosystems (stages of succession, cover type, etc.) present in each park. The initial inventory, and/or historical surveys, will serve as a baseline, and subsequent samples will be used to determine if bird populations are changing over time. It will be important to select key species to concentrate on since it will be impossible to adequately sample all bird species present. These would be species that respond to desired ecosystem conditions and species that can be reliably inventoried. Since forest habitats may be transitioning through various successional stages changes in bird populations would be expected to reflect habitat changes. However, if bird populations are changing to a non-desirable state (e.g. dominance by one or a few species, loss of critical species, rapid colonization by exotic species, etc.) it will be a cause for concern.

Limitations of Data and Monitoring: Bird sampling requires that trained observers be available in order to maintain consistency. In addition, studies of this nature require long-term commitment, and therefore, are expensive to conduct. Analysis and statistical inferences from bird survey data are often limited by the inability to take large samples and the low number of observations that characterize rare, but important species.

Key References:

Beard, G. R., W. A. Scott, and J. K. Adamson. 1999. The value of consistent methodology in long-term environmental monitoring. Environmental Monitoring and Assessment 54:239-258.

Bradford, D. F., S. E. Franson, A. C. Neale, D. T. Heggem, G. R. Miller, and G. E. Canterbury. 1998. Bird species assemblages as indicators of biological integrity in Great Basin rangeland. Environmental Monitoring and Assessment 49:1-22.

Cam, E., J. R. Sauer, J. D. Nichols, J. E. Hines, and C. H. Flather. 2000. Geographic analysis of species richness and community attributes of forest birds from survey data in the mid-atlantic integrated assessment region. Environmental Monitoring and Assessment 63:81-94.

Conner, R. N., and J. G. Dickson. 1997. Relationships between bird communities and forest age, structure, species composition and fragmentation in the West Gulf Coastal Plain. Texas Journal of Science 49(3):123-138.

Franzreb, K. E., and K. V. Rosenberg. 1997. Are forest birds declining? Status assessment from the Southern Appalachians and Northeastern Forests. Trans. 62nd North American Wildlife and Natural Resources Conference. Pp. 264-279.

Jones, K. B., A. C. Neale, M. S. Nash, K. H. Ritters, J. D. Wickham, R. V. O'Neill, and R. D. Van Remortel. 2000. Landscape correlations of breeding birds species richness across the United States Mid-Atlantic Region. Environmental Monitoring and Assessment 63:159-174.

Kilgo, J. C., K. E. Franzred, S. A. Gauthreaux, Jr., K. V. Miller, and B. R. Chapman. 2000. Effects of long-term forest management on a regional avifauna. Studies in Avian Biology 21:81-86.

Mikusinski, G., M. Gromadzki, and P. Chylarecki. 2001. Woodpeckers as indicators of forest bird diversity. Conservation Biology 15(1):208-217.

O'Connell, T. J., L. E. Jackson, and R. P. Brooks. 2000. Bird guilds as indicators of ecological condition in the central Appalachians. Ecological Applications 10(6):1706-1721.

Simons, T. R., K. N. Rabenold, D. A. Buehler, J. A. Collazo, and K. E. Franzreb. 1999. The role of indicator species: neotropical migratory song birds. *In* Peine, J.D., ed., Ecosystem Management for Sustainability. CRC Press LLC.

Smith, K. G., M. Mlodinow, J. S. Self, T. M. Haggerty, and T. R. Hocut. 2004. Birds of upland oak forests in the Arkansas Ozarks: present community structure and potential impacts of burning, borers, and forestry practices. *In* Spetich, M.A., ed., Upland oak ecology symposium: history, current conditions, and sustainability. USDA Forest Service. Gen. Tech. Rep. SRS-73. Pp. 311.

Yahner, R. H., B. D. Ross, G. S. Keller, and D. S. Klute. 2001. Comprehensive inventory program for birds at six Pennsylvania National Parks. National Park Service. Tech. Rep. NRTR-01/084. Pp. 63.

Related Environmental Issues and Linked Vital Signs: National parks are often islands that have been engulfed in a sea of private land. Activities that are on-going on adjacent land (timbering, surface mining, urban development, farming, etc.) can have a profound effect on the national park, and this is especially true regarding impact on bird populations. Breeding bird populations are also strongly linked to plant community structure and demography (VS20), which in turn can be affected by invasive plants, insects and diseases (VS18), and white-tailed deer (VS38).

Overall Assessment: Birds are a resource that is important to visitors of ERMN parks, and breeding bird populations are very sensitive to their habitat (quality, structure, etc.). Considerable historic data exist on breeding bird populations, some of which is specific to particular ERMN parks, but several parks lack site-specific data. An annual monitoring scheme is recommended that will allow for tracking changes in density of critical species and guilds, as well as to observe overall species richness. Because bird inventories are difficult, require trained observers, and must be maintained annually, a major commitment of personnel and funds will be required by the ERMN.

Level 1 ► Biological Integrity
    Level 2 ► Focal Species or Communities
        Level 3 ► Terrestrial Invertebrates (VS34)

Brief Description: The vital sign dealing with "Terrestrial Invertebrates" has to do with species of micro- and macro-invertebrates in the ERMN parks. These species include a variety of insects, arachnids, and other species. A large number of invertebrate species are involved in the processes of litter and woody debris breakdown. Others consume living plant biomass (defoliators, sap feeders, seed insects, wood and bark borers, etc.) and others are involved in processes such as pollination, spore dissemination, and seed dispersal. Diversity and abundance of invertebrates, to a large extent, reflects the diversity and health of host species and food sources; therefore, these species serve as indirect indicators of ecosystem health (Kermen et al. 1993; Taylor and Doran 2001). Certain species may serve a role as especially good indicators of overall ecosystem health and diversity. These include ground beetles (Rainio and Niemela 2003) and tiger beetles (Pearson and Cassola 1992). Changes in abundance and diversity of sensitive invertebrate species should serve as an index to changes in overall ecosystem states and therefore will serve to alert park managers to these changing conditions.

Significance/Justification: Terrestrial invertebrates, by far, represent the most numerous and diverse taxa in forest ecosystems. Not only do they serve as indicators of ecosystem condition, but many species perform vital ecosystem functions such as shredding of leaf litter, pollination, seed dispersal, soil aeration, etc, while others serve as food sources for organisms at higher tropic levels. Diversity of species like butterflies also can also serve as indicators of ecosystem changes, such as global warming and rainfall patterns (Pollard 1998). Because of their diversity and ubiquitous occurrence terrestrial invertebrates are very important functional components of terrestrial ecosystems and useful indicators of ecosystem health.

Proposed Metrics: Because of the great diversity and richness of terrestrial invertebrates, from a practical viewpoint it is useful to focus on *indicator taxa*. Kerr, Sugar and Packer (2000) found that species of Lepidoptera were suited to this purpose in oak savannahs in Ontario. As a refinement to this approach, Oliver and Beattie (1996) suggested combining the use of indicator taxa with the identification of appropriate sampling schemes (timing, methods) to maximize the information gained while minimizing the effort required for inventories. The appropriate metrics are measures of diversity (richness, evenness, etc.), density, and importance, and should be tracked over time and/or compared with existing baseline data.

Prospective Method(s) and Frequency of Measurement: Initially, decisions will need to be made to determine which taxa of terrestrial invertebrates will be focused on. This decision will depend on which ones are good "indicator taxa" and/or are functionally important to the parks. Once this decision is made, an initial inventory should be conducted to determine the density, distribution, and diversity of the selected taxa in the ERMN parks in order to establish a baseline. Sampling should be stratified proportional to the types of ecosystems (stages of succession, cover type, etc.) present in each park. Future monitoring (probably on a yearly or biennial basis) will be used to determine if populations are changing over time. Using the "indicator taxa" approach should allow the manager to extrapolate to other organisms and to use the data to assess overall ecosystem health. Since forest ecosystems are dynamic, it is reasonable to expect different populations of invertebrates in different ecosystems

Limitations of Data and Monitoring: Perhaps the sheer diversity, discontinuity, and density of invertebrate populations are limitations in and of themselves. Thoroughly sampling these populations is a difficult task and, if sampling of all species present is necessary, it would be virtually impossible, and very expensive.

Key References:

Haskell, D. G. 2000. Effects of forest roads on macro invertebrate soil fauna of the southern Appalachian Mountains. Conservation Biology 14(1):57-63.

Kerr, J. T., A. Sugar, and L. Packer. 2000. Indicator taxa, rapid biodiversity assessment, and nestedness in an endangered ecosystem. Conservation Biology 14(6):1726-1734.

Kremen, C., R. K. Colwell, T. L. Erwin, D. D. Murphy, R. F. Noss, and M. A. Sanyjayan. 1993. Terrestrial arthropod assemblages: their use in conservation planning. Conservation Biology 7(4):796-808.

Mudrick, D. A., M. Hoosein, R. R. Hicks, Jr., and E. C. Townsend. 1994. Decomposition of litter in an Appalachian forest: effects of leaf species, aspect, slope position and time. Forest Ecol. and Mgt. 68:231-250.

Oliver, I., and A. J. Beattie. 1996. Designing a cost-effective invertebrate survey: a test of methods for rapid assessment of biodiversity. Ecological Applications 6(2):594-607.

Pearson, D. L., and F. Cassola. 1992. World-wide species richness patterns of tiger beetles (Coleoptera: Cicindelidae): Indicator taxon for biodiversity and conservation studies. Conservation Biology 6(3):376-391.

Pollard, E. 1988. Temperature, rainfall, and butterfly numbers. Journal of Applied Ecology 25:819-828.

Rainio, J., and J. Niemelä. 2003. Ground beetles (Coleoptera: Carabidae) as bioindicators. Biodiversity and Conservation 12:487-506.

Roy, D. B., P. Rothery, D. Moss, E. Pollard, and J. A. Thomas. 2001. Journal of Animal Ecology 70:201-217.

Taylor, R. J., and N. Doran. 2001. Use of terrestrial invertebrates as indicators of the ecological sustainability of forest management under the Montreal Process. Journal of Insect Conservation 5:221-231.

Related Environmental Issues and Linked Vital Signs: Because of their great numbers and diversity, terrestrial invertebrates have a profound effect on many aspects of the ecosystem. Their populations may be affected by atmospheric pollution (VS1, VS2) or they may interact with such things as weather and climate (VS4). Even soil properties such as compaction (VS11) can be ameliorated by the presence of some terrestrial invertebrates. The leaf shredder populations are very much a function of the type of litter produced (Mudrick et. al 1994), which in turn is a function of the overstory community present (VS20). Litter decomposition and nutrient cycling (VS60, VS61) are affected by shredder populations and these, in turn, affect bio-productivity (VS59). A number of invertebrates function in ways that affect the overall ecosystem function. For example, invasive insects (VS18) like gypsy moth pose a significant threat to ecosystem health in the ERMN. Many other invertebrates are contributory to ecosystem health, such as pollinators, earthworms, etc.

Overall Assessment: Terrestrial invertebrates are very diverse and important to the functioning of the ecosystems in the ERMN. Some, like introduced insect pests, are detrimental as well. Monitoring the overall diversity and the populations of selected invertebrate species should yield information that is valuable to park managers. In order to expedite the process it will be necessary to monitor "indicator taxa" and a stratified sampling scheme should be devised that will monitor invertebrates in the various forest cover types and successional stages present. Once a baseline has been established, monitoring on an annual or biennial frequency should provide managers with a perspective on the maintenance of diversity among invertebrates in the parks, which should serve as an indicator of ecosystem health.

Level 1 ▶ Biological Integrity
    Level 2 ▶ Focal Species or Communities
        Level 3 ▶ White-tailed Deer (VS38)

Brief Description: "White-tailed Deer" refers to the populations of *Odocoileus virginianus* residing in the ERMN parks and their impact on the ecosystems. White-tailed deer populations have grown astronomically throughout the eastern United States since the turn of the Twentieth Century, at which time they had been almost extirpated from many areas (Cote et al. 2004). The rapid increase is due to a combination of factors, including 1) increase in habitat through re-growth of abandoned fields and cut-over forests, 2) regulations prohibiting doe hunting and better enforcement of regulations, and 3) elimination of the natural predators of white-tailed deer. The urbanization of many areas has been a contributory factor, in that hunting is excluded from developments and there is a general loss of the "hunting culture" typical of rural areas. Furthermore, deer do well in suburban situations. Deer have been described as a "keystone herbivore" by Waller and Anderson (1997), owing to the profound impact that they have on forest ecosystems, including limiting the regeneration of preferred woody or herbaceous browse species (Rooney and Waller 2003). In fact, one of the factors causing the apparent poor regeneration of oaks in the Eastern United States is white-tailed deer herbivory (Healy 1997). In the ERMN parks, as well as the National Park System as a whole, white-tailed deer have been identified as a major disruptive factor to the ecosystems.

Significance/Justification: White-tailed deer impact in the eastern deciduous forest region is one of the most significant causes of structural ecosystem changes, affecting everything from wild flowers and herbs to songbirds (Anderson 1994; DeCalesta 1994; Russel, Zippin and Fowler 2001). Deer can alter plant species diversity (Rooney and Dress 1997) and contribute to the local loss of endangered plants in areas where deer are overpopulated. Deer are a primary stressor in ecosystems where they are overpopulated and their impact is primarily on processes such as regeneration (Jones et al. 1993). The ERMN parks generally have high deer populations that are affecting forest regeneration, understory diversity, and other ecosystem processes. Fortunately, a substantial body of knowledge exists regarding the population levels of deer which are likely to cause irreparable harm to forest ecosystems (Marquis 1981). It is also possible to control harvesting of deer on National Park Service land, as long as it conforms to state regulations. Thus, the Park Service has an opportunity to manage herd size with the goal of keeping populations below damaging thresholds.

Proposed Metrics: The most commonly-used metric used to describe deer is density expressed as number per unit area, typically number per square mile. The recommendation to managers is to maintain deer populations below 15–20 animals per square mile to maintain low impact on forest regeneration (Marquis and Twery 1992). In addition to the deer density, the extent of deer browsing should be documented in forest understories, as well as the type and frequency of occurrence of forest regeneration present. The latter may be indicative of deer impact, especially if regeneration is virtually absent or composed exclusively of species that are not preferred by deer.

Prospective Method(s) and Frequency of Measurement: There are several standard methods used to inventory deer numbers. Direct counts from deer drives, pellet group counts, and nighttime aerial infrared photography are examples of these. Perhaps the most practical method is pellet group counts conducted in the spring after snow melt (Eberhardt and Van Etten 1956). This method is less expensive than the others and, although it is not as accurate for predicting absolute population numbers, yearly pellet inventories are quite useful in demonstrating population trends. For browsing surveys, understory subplots can be evaluated for browsing intensity of woody and herbaceous plants by species and size class. A somewhat subjective system in which understory plants are categorized as unbrowsed, lightly browsed (<50% of tips), moderately browsed (>50% of tips), and heavily browsed (100% of tips) works well and is simple to perform in the field. A deer census should be conducted at intervals of no more than five years, and understory inventories should be conducted approximately every two years. Perhaps a good compromise is to monitor pellet counts and understory annually using a network of permanent plots, and supplement this with a nighttime infrared survey on a 5-year interval. This would allow for the observation of year-to-year variation, while placing the pellet estimates on a firmer basis relative to the actual population density.

Limitations of Data and Monitoring: As previously indicated, pellet group surveys are limited as to their accuracy. Deer tend to follow predetermined trails in the forest and their pellet groups are clustered around these areas and areas where heavy feeding occurs. In order to obtain good population estimates a large number of sample points is necessary, and finding and counting pellet groups is difficult.

Key References:

Anderson, C. A. 1994. Height of white-flowered trillium (*Trillium grandiflorum*) as an index of deer browsing intensity. Ecological Applications 4(1):104-109.

Augustine, D. J., and L. E. Frehlich. 1998. Effects of white-tailed deer on populations of an understory forb in fragmented deciduous forests. Conservation Biology 12(5):995-1004.

Cote, S. D., T. P. Rooney, J-P. Tremblay, C. Dussault, and D. M. Waller. 2004. Ecological impacts of deer overabundance. Annual Review of Ecology, Evolution, and Systematics 35:113-147.

DeCalesta, D. S. 1994. Effect of white-tailed deer on songbirds within managed forests in Pennsylvania. Journal of Wildlife Management 58:711-717.

Eberhardt, L., and R. C. Van Etten. 1956. Evaluation of pellet group count as a deer census method. J. Wildlife Mgt. 20(1):70-74.

Halls, L. K. (ed.). 1984. White-tailed deer: ecology and management. Stackpole Books. Harrisburg, PA. 870 pp.

Healy, W. M. 1997. Influence of deer on the structure and composition of oak forests in central Massachusetts. *In*: The Science of Overabundance: Deer Ecology and Population Management (W. J. McShea, H. b. Underwood and J. H. Rappole, eds.). Smithsonian Institution Press. Washington, DC. pp 249-266.

Horsley, S. B., S. L. Stout, and D. S. DeCalesta. 2003. White-tailed deer impact on the vegetation dynamics of a northern hardwood forest. Ecological Applications 13(1):98-118.

Jones, S. B., D. DeCalesta, and S. E. Chunko. 1993. White-tails are changing our woodlands. Am. For. Dec.:20-25.

Marquis, D. A. 1981. Effect of deer browsing on timber in Allegheny hardwood forests of northwestern Pennsylvania. The impact of deer browsing on Allegheny hardwood regeneration. USDA Forest Service, Res. Rep. NE-57.

Marquis, D. A., and M. J. Twery. 1992. Decision-making for natural regeneration in the northern forest ecosystem. *In:* Proc.: Oak Regeneration: Serious Problems, Practical Recommendations, D. L. Loftis and C. E. McGee (eds.). USDA, Forest Serv. Gen. Tech. Rep. SE-84:156-173.

McShea, W. J., and J. H. Rappole. 2000. Managing the abundance and diversity of breeding bird populations through manipulation of deer populations. Conservation Biology 14:1161-1170.

Miller, S. G., S. P. Bratton, and J. Hadidian. 1992. Impacts of white-tailed deer on endangered plants. Nat. Areas J. 12:67-74.

Porter, W. F. 1991. White-tailed deer in eastern ecosystems: implications for management and research in national parks. Natural Resources Report NPS/NRSUNY/NRR-91/05. National Park Service. Denver, CO. 57 pp.

Redding, J. 1995. History of deer population trends and forest cutting on the Allegheny National Forest. *In* Gottschalk, K. W. and Fosbroke, S. C. L., editors. Proc. 10th Central Hardwood Forest Conf.. USDA Genl. Tech. Rept. NE-197.

Rooney, T. P., and W. J. Dress. 1997. Patterns of plant diversity in overbrowsed primary and mature secondary hemlock-northern hardwood forest stands. Journal of the Torrey Botanical Society 124(1):43-51.

Rooney, T. P., and D. N. Waller. 2003. Direct and indirect effects of white-tailed deer in forest ecosystems. Forest Ecology and Management 181:165-176.

Russell, R. L., D. B. Zippin, and N. L. Fowler. 2001. Effects of white-tailed deer (*Odocoileus virginianus*) on plants, plant populations and communities: a review. American Midland Naturalist 146(1):1-26.

Waller, D. M., and W. S. Alverson. 1997. The white-tailed deer: a keystone herbivore. Wildl. Soc. Bull. 25(2):217-226.

Level 1 ▶ Biological Integrity
 Level 2 ▶ Focal Species or Communities
  Level 3 ▶ Reptiles and Amphibians (VS48)

Brief Description: "Reptiles and Amphibians" refer to the populations of herptofauna occurring in the ERMN parks. Species of reptiles and amphibians of interest include frogs, toads, turtles, terrapins, salamanders, lizards, and snakes. Herptofauna, especially frogs and salamanders, have been reported to be in decline worldwide and have been identified as indicators of ecosystem stress (Welsh and Oliver 1998). In part, this derives from the fact that the exothermic herps are intimately dependent upon their environment for heat and food; even to the extent of absorbing water and gases through their skin. Certain species (notably snakes and lizards) seem to prefer open and dry habitats, while salamanders and frogs prefer moist habitats (Crosswhite, Fox and Thill 2004). Impacts of global climate change, atmospheric deposition, and air pollution would most likely be apparent in herptofaunal communities before they would in other sectors of the terrestrial ecosystem. Therefore, the health and diversity of herptofauna in ERMN parks should be monitored closely in order to provide indications of ecosystem changes.

Significance/Justification: Herptofauna are relatively diverse in the ERMN region, being represented by 35–50 species (Green and Pauley 1987; Kilpatrick et al. 2004). Because of their environmental sensitivity these species represent potentially good indicators of ecosystem health. Although not specific to the individual ERMN parks, there exists a comprehensive compilation of data regarding herptofauna in the eastern deciduous and Appalachian forest regions (Pauley 2001) which can serve as a historic background for comparison with present and future populations.

Metrics: Relative density and diversity (richness) are the commonly used measures to describe herptofauna in forested ecosystems. For relative density, number of a particular species compared to the total number of all species is the metric of choice. Because of the difficulty of sampling it may be hard to find certain herp species, especially at times of the year when they are inactive or hibernating, so sampling should focus on areas of prime habitat and should be conducted at times when target species are active.

Prospective Method(s) and Frequency of Measurement: There are a variety of sampling methods used to collect and inventory herptofauna (Corn and Bury 1990). For snakes and terrapins, drift fences leading to pitfalls or double-ended funnels are frequently used. Frogs, newts, and toads can be trapped with funnel traps, either in aquatic or terrestrial habitat; again, the trapping method should conform to the target species and the activity phase they are in at a given time, since many species of amphibians have both terrestrial and aquatic phases. Salamanders are usually inventoried using coverboards (Felix, Wang and Schweitzer 2004), and here again, sampling should be conducted at times of the year when salamanders are active, and not during periods of extended dry weather or extended wet weather. Herptofauna sampling should be stratified by broad forest cover types (conifer, oak forests, northern hardwoods, mesophytic hardwoods) and stages of ecosystem development (recently-disturbed, second-growth, old-growth). Since there are several species of herptofauna to inventory it may be difficult, time-consuming, and expensive to attempt to inventory them all each year. Using a staggered schedule over a period of 3–5 years the ERMN could monitor part of the species each year. In so doing, annual inventories can be conducted for species having similar habits—those that can be inventoried using the same or similar methods. At the end of a full cycle the first species group inventoried would be re-sampled, and over a period of several cycles trends in relative density of individual species and overall diversity can be established.

Limitations of Data and Monitoring: Most species of herptofauna are small in size and active only during part of the year in temperate forests. Some live in the soil or beneath leaf litter or rocks, therefore, sampling must be done in ways that accumulate them (drift fences, coverboards, etc.). Exact population numbers are difficult to obtain since it is impossible to obtain a census of all individuals in a particular land area. This is one reason herpetologists often rely on relative density and diversity when describing the herptofaunal community of an area. In the case of threatened and endangered species, such as the cheat mountain salamander, the fact that they are rare complicates sampling and makes it necessary to concentrate sampling efforts in areas of prime habitat, which may in itself pose a threat to the species.

Key References:
Corn, P. S., and R. B. Bury. 1990. Sampling methods for terrestrial amphibians and reptiles. USDA Forest Service. Gen. Tech. Rep. PNW-GTR-256.

Crosswhite, D. L., S. F. Fox, and R. E. Thill. 2004. Herpetological habitat relations in the Ouachita Mountains, Arkansas. USDA Forest Service. Gen. Tech. Rep. SRS-74.

Felix, Z. I., Y. Wang, and C. J. Schweitzer. 2004. Relationships between herpetofaunal community structure and varying levels of overstory tree retention in northern Alabama: first-year results. USDA Forest Service. Proceedings of the 12th biennial southern silvicultural research conference. Gen. Tech. Rep. SRS-71. 594 pp.

Ford, W. M, M. A. Menzel, and R. H. Odom. 2002. Elevation, aspect, and cove size effects on southern Appalachian salamanders. Southeastern Naturalist 1(4):15-324.

Green, N. B., and T. K. Pauley. 1987. Amphibians and Reptiles in West Virginia. University of Pittsburgh Press. 241 pp.

Greenberg, C. H. 2001. Response of reptile and amphibian communities to canopy gaps created by wind disturbance in the southern Appalachians. Forest Ecology and Management 148:135-144.

Harper, C. A., and D. C. Guynn, Jr. 1999. Factors affecting salamander density and distribution withing four forest types in the southern Appalachian Mountains. Forest Ecology and Management 114:245-252.

Jung, R. E., S. Droege, J. R. Sauer, and R. B. Landy. 2000. Evaluation of terrestrial and streamside salamander monitoring techniques at Shenandoah National Park. Environmental Monitoring and Assessment 63:65-79.

Kilpatrick, E. S., D. B. Kubacz, D. C. Guynn, Jr., J. D. Lanham, and T. A. Waldrop. 2004. The effects of prescribed burning and thinning on herptofauna and small mammals in the upper piedmont of South Carolina: preliminary results of the national fire and fire surrogate study. USDA Forest Service. Proceedings of the 12th biennial southern silvicultural research conference, Gen. Tech. Rep. SRS-71, p. 594.

Pauley, T. K. 1987. Range of the Cheat Mountain Salamander. Herpetological Review 18(2):39.

Pauley, T. K. 1993. report of upland vertebrates in the New River Gorge National River. Report to the New River Gorge National River, Glen Jean, WV. 3 volumes.

Pauley, T. K. 1994. Impact of Deer and Silvicultural Treatment on Forest Amphibians in Northwestern Pennsylvania. USDA-Forest Service.

Pauley, T. K. 2001. Amphibians and Reptiles in West Virginia. West Virginia Encyclopedia. West Virginia Historical and Cultural Center.

Pauley, T. K. 2000. Amphibians and Reptiles in wetlands of the central Appalachians. Proceedings of the West Virginia Academy of Science.

Russell, K. R., T. B. Wigley, W. M. Baughman, H. G. Hanlin, and W. M. Ford. 2004. Responses of southeastern amphibians and reptiles to forest management: a review. *In* Rauscher, H. M., and Johnsen, K. (eds.), Southern Forest Science: Past, Present, and Future. USDA Forest Service. GTR SRS-75. Pp. 319-334.

Waldron, J. L., T. K. Pauley, Z. I. Felix, W. J. Humphries, and A. J. Longenecker. 2000. The herpetofauna of the Bluestone National Wild and Scenic River. Proceedings of the West Virginia Academy of Science.

Walters, J. R. 1991. Application of ecological principles to the management of endangered species: the case of the red-cockaded woodpecker. Annual Review of Ecology and Systematics 22:505-523.

Welsh H. H., Jr., and S. Droege. 2001. A case for using plethodontid salamanders for monitoring biodiversity and ecosystem integrity of North American forests. Conservation Biology 15(3):558-569.

Welsh, H., and L. Ollivier. 1998. Stream amphibians as indicators of ecosystem stress: a case study from California's redwoods. Ecological Applications 8:1118-1132.

Related Environmental Issues and Linked Vital Signs: Herptofauna, because of their proximity to the soil and dependence on ambient moisture and temperature, are very sensitive to climatic effects (VS1- VS5). In addition, soil and geologic conditions (parent material, soil texture, stone content, compaction, etc. have a profound effect of herptofauna (VS11, VS12). The overstory community also has an important effect on herptofauna, since many species live in the organic soil layers which are produced from decomposing organic matter produced by the trees (VS20). Terrestrial invertebrates (VS 34) constitute a major food source for many herps (VS34), and some herptofauna are among the state and federal T&E species (VS49, VS50). Finally, herptofauna are particularly susceptible to damage from visitor over-usage (VS54). And because of their limited mobility, herptofauna may be especially sensitive to changes in the land cover or land use (VS57). Herptofauna , because of their sensitivity, diversity, and links to many other vital signs, make good indicators of ecosystem health and stability.

Overall Assessment: Herptofauna represent a diverse group of organisms that have experienced worldwide declines in recent decades. They are generally acknowledged to be sensitive to changes in their environment, including climate change as well as atmospheric pollution. These species could provide ERMN park managers with an early warning system for ecological degradation. Because of their life histories and habitat characteristics herptofauna are difficult to survey and monitor, but a well-planned system of sampling should provide good data for establishing trends in relative densities and diversity, which should, in turn, be a valuable descriptor for use by park managers.

Level 1 ▶ Human Use
    Level 2 ▶ Visitor and Recreation Use
        Level 3 ▶ Visitor Usage (VS54)

Brief Description: "Visitor Usage" refers to the impact on ERMN parks that is caused by human usage, including direct impacts such as soil compaction and devegetation, as well as indirect effects such as pollution caused by auto emissions and human waste. Because of the federal mandate to National Parks to preserve unique resources and natural areas for the benefit of the American people, a paradox exists, such that over-use runs the risk of destroying the very resources that people come to use. Parks in the ERMN area are generally within a day's drive of more than 50% of Americans, therefore, they are heavily used by visitors, and this usage will likely increase in the future. Activities such as rock climbing are especially prone to do damage since cliffline areas are a relatively rare component of the landscape and the types of flora and fauna associated with them is often unique to these rare sites (McMillan and Larson 2002; Eagles 2001; Kelly and Larson 1997). Trails concentrate the impact of users (which can mitigate the general impact of dispersed use), but trails must be well planned, appropriately located, regulated as to type and amount of use, and well maintained in order to prevent excessive damage (Weaver and Dale 1978). The dilemma presented to park managers is to determine how to preserve the valuable resources in national parks while at the same time making them available to the public.

Significance/Justification: Using Manion's (1981) classification of ecosystem stressors visitor usage would fall into the category of a contributing factor. The ecological impact of visitors depends very much on the number and type of visitors, the sensitivity of the resource(s) being affected, and the overall environmental context. For example, a large number of visitors riding ATV's in a wetland site would have a much higher impact than the same number of birders visiting an upland forest site on foot. But even activities that would appear benign at first glance may cause damage, especially when they occur repeatedly over the long term. It is important for the ERMN park managers to assess the short-term and long-term impacts of visitors and to manage these impacts in order to minimize ecosystem damage.

Proposed Metrics: Determining visitor impacts is a difficult task, especially when there is little opportunity to develop controlled experiments. For example, the impact of whitewater activities on the flat-rock communities of the New and Gauley Rivers may be difficult to ascertain, since there is no suitable experimental control. Indeed, even if pre-post information existed, it would be of limited value since other things are probably changing in the environment over any given interval of time. Cessford and Muhar (2004) describe the range of options available for visitor monitoring in National Parks, but simply documenting the numbers and attributes of visitors may not adequately address the type and level of damage they are causing. In many cases, inventories of sensitive plants and animals in high-use areas will be a required component of any visitor-impact monitoring program in order to link visitor usage with environmental damage. Thus metrics such as visitor person-days will need to be associated with ecosystem metrics such as relative density and diversity of sensitive plant and animal species in order to see the complete picture.

Prospective Method(s) and Frequency of Measurement: In order to establish the resource impacts that occur as a result of visitor usage, controlled experiments are the best option, using several replications of "test" sites that are experiencing high visitor pressure and a similar set of "control" sites which are receiving little or no impact over the same interval. In order for such an experiment to be valid, the two sets of sites should be as similar as possible, and have a similar history of disturbance prior to the initiation of the experiment. Such an experiment is seldom practical since the "test" areas are probably sites that have had historically high visitation rates because they possess unique and interesting attributes (e. g. a scenic viewing areas or waterfalls). A practical alternative is the use of so-called before-after-control-impact-pair (BACIP) designs (Stewart-Oaten and Murdoch 1986). In these studies control and test areas are monitored prior to the impact for several years and then again following the initiation of visitor impact. This is especially suitable where a new facility is being constructed in an area that has heretofore been relatively unaffected by visitors. Another method of establishing impact, that is especially suited to sites where visitor use is concentrated, is the installation of transects radiating away from the high-use area. This is especially suited to campsites, trails, picnic areas, etc. The variables to monitor for impact in any of these studies would be those suspected to receive either direct or indirect impact (species diversity, soil compaction, presence or absence of sensitive species, etc.). At such time as an impact is apparent the park manager may wish to establish limits on the number and/or timing of permitted visits. Wang and Manning (1999) describe a modeling tool that could be used to set "carrying-capacity" limitations on park usage, which may be a reasonable approach to managing visitor impacts.

Limitations of Data and Monitoring: As indicated above, there is an almost endless combination of types of resources/ecosystems, types of visitor impacts, and sensitivities of ecosystem components, so any viable monitoring system for visitor impacts should be focused on sites where impacts are most likely to occur. Many of the standard experimental designs and sampling methods are of limited value in developing visitor impact data, so methods like the BACIP design are required. These methods may not be as robust as statistical designs where strict control over the experimental conditions is possible. Finally, because of the difficulty in acquiring data and the number of potential ecosystem impacts, visitor impact analysis can be expensive and time consuming.

Key References:

Cessford, G., and A. Muhar. 2004. Monitoring options for visitor numbers in national parks and natural areas. Journal for Nature Conservation 11(4):240-250.

Cole, D. N. 2000. Biophysical impacts of wildland recreation use. *In* Gartner, W.C. and Lime, D. W., eds. *Trends in Outdoor Recreation, Leisure, and Tourism*. Oxon, UK: CABI Publishing. Pp. 257-264.

Cole, D. N., and V. Wright. 2003. Wilderness visitors and recreation impacts: baseline data available for the twentieth century conditions. USDA Forest Service. Gen. Tech. Rep. RMRS-GTR-117. Pp. 52.

Cook, C., D. Andrus, and M. R. Neil. 2004. Environmental response to natural resource management regimes: twenty years of visitor impacts in the Bob Marshall Wilderness. *In* Murdy, James, comp., ed. Proceedings of the 2003 Northeastern Recreation Research Symposium. 2003 April 6-8. Bolton Landing, NY. Gen. Tech. Rep. NE-316. Newtown

Square, PA: U.S. Department of Agriculture, Forest Service, Northeastern Research Station: 246-251.

Eagles, P. F. J. 2001. Evolution of the concept of visitor use in parks. Industry and Environment 24(3-4):65-67.

English, D. B. K., S. M. Kocis, S. J. Zarnoch, and J. R. Arnold. 2002. Forest Service National Visitor Use Monitoring Process: Research Methods Documentation. USDA Forest Service, Gen. Tech. Rep. SRS-54. Pp. 14.

English, D. B. K., S. M. Kocis, S. J. Zarnoch, and L. Warren. 2004. The effectiveness of visitation proxy variables in improving recreation use estimates for the USDA Forest Service. Journal of Nature Conservation 11(4):332-338.

Kelly, P. E., and D. W. Larson. 1997. Effects of rock climbing on populations of presettlement eastern white ceder (Thuja occidentalis) on cliffs of the Niagara Escarpment, Canada. Conservation Biology 11(5):1125-1132.

Manion, P. D. Forest Disease Concepts. Prentice- Hall. Englwood Cliffs, N. J. 399 pp.

McMilan, M. A., and D. W. Larson. 2002. Effects of rock climbing on the vegetation of the Niagara Escarpment in Southern Ontario, Canada. Conservation Biology 16(2):389-398.

Stewart-Oaten, A., and W. W. Murdoch. 1986. Environmental impact assessment: "pseudoreplication" in time? Ecology 67(4):929-940.

Symmonds, M.C., and W. E. Hammitt. 2000. Managing recreational trail environments for mountain bike user preferences. Environmental Management 25(5):549-564.

Wang, B., and R. E. Manning. 1999. Computer simulation modeling for recreation management: a study on carriage road use in Acadia National Park, Maine, USA. Environmental Management 23(2):193-203.

Weaver, T., and D. Dale. 1978. Trampling effects of hikers, motorcycles and horses in meadows and forests. Journal of Applied Ecology 15(2):451-457.

Related Environmental Issues and Linked Vital Signs: Visitor impacts are especially significant regarding soil compaction/erosion (VS11), which, in turn, can affect soil biota (VS12) and terrestrial invertebrates (VS34). Visitors are likely to have impacts on certain unique resources such as rimrock pine communities, clifflines, and cliffline communities (VS21, VS8, VS22), which, in turn, can affect cliff-dwelling species such as peregrine falcons, Allegheny woodrats (VS35), and bats (VS33). Visitors also can create noise pollution (VS55) as well as initiate changes in land use patterns, bio-productivity, litter dynamics, and nutrient cycling (VS 57, 58, 59, 60, 61).

Overall Assessment: Because national parks are sites set aside for the use and enjoyment of the public, a paradox exists between preserving the resources and allowing people to use them. Therefore, park managers must walk a tightrope between permitting use and preserving the environment. Visitors to parks have the potential of causing widespread damage, including destruction of habitat, local loss of species, and soil compaction and erosion. The park managers need data to determine the extent of visitor damage and to enable them to set carrying-capacity limits in areas where use threatens important resources. Methods for assessing visitor use and visitor impacts are often difficult and expensive to apply and should be targeted to sensitive resources in high-use areas.

Brief Description: "Landscape Dynamics" refers to the states and distribution of the various dominant cover types, as they exist within a landscape mosaic. In addition to the current pattern, historic patterns (Braun 1950) should be considered, as well as trends and changes in landscape patterns. These changes can be useful indicators of the natural and human-caused forces acting upon the landscape (Alig and Butler 2004). Turner et al. (2003) examined the landscape-level changes in the Appalachian region (including much of the ERMN) and found that during the four-decade interval from 1950 to 1990 the amount of forest cover increased and fragmentation decreased, but they cautioned that recent housing development in the region may offset many of these gains. Human impacts are a critical element in the changing landscapes of the ERMN and Ritters et al. (2000) indicate that land cover information provides a mechanism to place humans into ecological assessments.

Significance/Justification: Humans are one of the primary drivers in landscape-level changes (Ritters et al. 2000). Historical occurrences such as agricultural clearing, agricultural abandonment, timbering, surface mining, forest fire control, predator eradication, hunting regulation, insect and disease introductions, and urban sprawl are all examples of how humans have contributed to landscape-level changes over the last hundred and fifty years. ERMN parks are, in effect, islands within an ever-changing mosaic of land, and changes outside the ERMN parks can potentially affect the ecological properties within the parks (Brosofske et al. 1999). Roads have a particularly significant fragmenting effect on terrestrial ecosystems (Forman 2000; Trombulak and Fressell 2004). Changes in landscape pattern can alter habitat for neotropical birds, mammals (Dijak and Thompson 2000), and forest wetlands (Gibbs 2000). Because land use patterns surrounding the ERMN are changing, and these changes have the potential for altering the ecological characteristics within the parks, it is important that park managers be aware of this process and how it is likely to affect them.

Proposed Metrics: Landscape ecology is a field that uses spatial analysis methods to evaluate the pattern of various land cover types at different spatial scales. Metrics include the proportion of a given landscape occurring in a particular cover type and indices of patchiness, fragmentation, connectivity, etc. These metrics can be used to compare among landscapes or to observe temporal changes in a single landscape.

Prospective Method(s) and Frequency of Measurement: Spatial analysis methods begin with imagery (aerial photography, satellite images, etc.) and databases (USGS topographic information, ownership, etc.). Image information requires interpretation in order to determine what the visual information represents. Interpretation can be facilitated by image enhancing methods such as digital color transformations. The resulting information is used to create a geographic information system (GIS) that incorporates multiple layers of spatial information, such as land use, ownership, cover type, topography, etc. Software packages are available that provide powerful tools for organizing, interpreting, and displaying the information. Spatial statistics can be used to analyze the data (Gardner et al. 1987), and models constructed using information from known landscapes can be used to predict the states of other landscapes (Trombulak and Frissell 2004).

Limitations of Data and Monitoring: A substantial amount of landscape-level information currently exists, much of which is public record, and therefore inexpensive to acquire. The problem with many available sources of images or spatial data is that they must be adapted to the specific use required (e.g., ERMN parks). The detail, scale, and type of imagery may not suit the specific purpose of the ERMN; thus, requiring that new and expensive data need to be gathered. The development of a system-wide GIS can be a daunting task, requiring either contractors or trained NPS employees to complete the work. Furthermore, as Li and Wu (2004) warn, landscape analysis often falls short of meeting its high expectations due to conceptual flaws in pattern analysis, inherent limitations of landscape indices, and improper use of pattern indices.

Key References:

Alig, R. J., and B. J. Butler. 2004. Area changes for forest cover types in the United States, 1952 to 1997, with projections to 2050. USDA Forest Service. Gen. Tech. Rep. PNW-GTR-613. Pp. 106.

Braun, E. L. 1950. Deciduous Forests of Eastern North America. The Blakiston Co. Philadelphia, PA.

Brosofske, K. D., J. Chen, T. R. Crow, and S. C. Saunders. 1999. Vegetation responses to landscape structure at multiple scales across a northern Wisconsin, USA pine barrens landscape. Plant ecology 143:203-218.

Dijak, W. D., and F. R. Thompson. 2000. Landscape and edge effects on the distribution of mammalian predators in Missouri. Journal of Wildlife Management 64(1):209-216.

Forman, R. T. T. 2000. Estimate of the area affected ecologically by the road system in the United States. Conservation Biology 14(1):31-35.

Gardner, R. H., B. T. Milne, M. G. Turner, and R. V. O'Neill. 1987. Neutral models for the analysis of broad-scale landscape pattern. Landscape Ecology 1(1):19-28.

Gibbs, J. P. 2000. Wetland loss and biodiversity conservation. Conservation Biology 14(1): 314-317.

Jones, K. B., A. C. Neale, T. G. Wade, J. D. Wickham, C. L. Cross, C. M. Edmonds, T. R. Loveland, M. S. Nash, K. H. Riitters, and E. R. Smith. 2001. Ecosystem Health 7(4):229-242.

Li, H., and J. Wu. 2004. Use and misuse of landscape indices. Landscape Ecology 19:389-399.

Pickett, S. T. A., and P. S. White. 1986. The ecology of natural disturbance and patch dynamics. Academic Press.

Ritters, K. H., J. D. Wickham, J. E. Vogelman, and K. B. Jones. 2000. National land-cover data. Ecology 81:604.

Trombulak, S. C., and C. A. Frissell. 2004. Review of ecological effects of roads on terrestrial and aquatic communities. Conservation Biology 14(1):18-30.

Turner, M. G., S. M. Pearson, P. Bolstad, and D. N. Wear. 2003. Effects of land-cover change on spatial pattern of forest communities in the Southern Appalachian Mountains (USA). Landscape Ecology 18:449-464.

Wear, D. N., and P. Bolstad. 1998. Land-use changes in southern Appalachian landscapes: spatial analysis and forecast evaluation. Ecosystems 1(6):575-594.

Related Environmental Issues and Linked Vital Signs: Landscape pattern is related to many environmental issues, particularly ones having to do with anthropogenic effects such as pollution, land use, settlement, etc. Landscape patterns are linked with almost all the vital signs identified for ERMN parks. Atmospheric and climatic patterns (VS1-VS4) vary across the landscape, and these factors, in turn, create patterns in vegetation and land use. Geology and soils (VS6-VS12) also contribute to landscape patterns, as well as do hydrologic features (VS14, VS15). Because human activities often are involved in the introduction of invasive species, and human habitation is part of the landscape pattern, the pattern of introduction of invasive species (VS18) often follows the patterns of human activity (transportation, settlement, etc.). Plant and animal communities (VS 20- VS48) are specifically adapted to their environment, which changes across the landscape. Visitor usage (VS54) can locally alter an ecosystem; thereby, imposing an anthropogenic pattern on the landscape. Finally, bio-productivity and nutrient dynamics (VS59, VS61) are specifically linked to the landscape pattern. In short, the pattern that exists on the landscape is a reflection of the sum of the abiotic, biotic, and anthropogenic factors that interact over it.

Overall Assessment: Landscape pattern is a result of the interaction of numerous factors (historic and present). ERMN parks are themselves part of a larger landscape and are affected by actions that take place beyond their boundaries. The discipline of landscape ecology has been developing in recent years and involves using imagery, data, technology, and statistical tools to analyze and interpret spatial information. ERMN managers can use these methods to assess current conditions in their parks as they relate to the larger landscape. Use of this tool may enable managers to anticipate changes and take remedial actions, when necessary.

Level 1 ▶ Ecosystem Pattern and Process
   Level 2 ▶ Primary Production
      Level 3 ▶ Primary Production/Biomass Production (VS59)

Brief Description: "Primary Production/Biomass Production" relates to primary productivity of terrestrial ecosystems and the factors that influence it. Primary productivity is a function of the site quality (available resources), the stage of development of the ecosystem, and the health of the ecosystem. Thus, for a given level of site quality and stage of development, primary productivity can be used as an indicator of ecosystem health. Primary productivity is often measured in terms of gross primary productivity (GPP), or more commonly as net primary productivity (NPP) which accounts for losses due to mortality. Various methods of measuring and/or modeling NPP have been developed. Some, such as Normalized Difference Vegetation Index and Enhanced Vegetation Index, use remotely-sensed data from satellite imagery (Weier and Herring 2005). Others utilize data from USDA, Forest Service Forest Inventory and Analysis (FIA) plots (Wharton and Raile 1984). In the absence of directly measured biomass data, models have been developed that can be used to predict the amount of biomass present, given certain information on site and forest conditions (Botkin, Janak and Wallis 1972; Running andd Gower 1991). These biomass accumulation models provide a baseline against which actual biomass production of a given ecosystem can be compared.

Significance/Justification: Primary production (NPP) is a fundamental property of ecosystems (Geiger et al. 2001). Biomass produced by autotrophs forms the foundation of the energy pyramid and sets basic limits on all higher trophic levels. The "direct factors" (resources) that determine potential bio-productivity are solar radiation, heat, available water, oxygen, carbon dioxide, and mineral nutrients (Hicks 1998). At some point, one or the other of these resources becomes a limiting factor and productivity of the ecosystem then becomes limited by the level of that resource. Ecosystems within landscapes have "expected norms" for productivity, therefore, any deviation from this may indicate a change in some ecosystem property. Therefore, tracking biomass production provides an important tool for ERMN park managers.

Proposed Metrics: Metrics for reporting biomass productivity generally take the form of a rate, such as weight per unit area per unit time (Kg/ha/yr). In some cases surrogate variables can be measured to estimate productivity. For example, Ryan (1991) suggested using litterfall to estimate below-ground carbon allocation and tissue nitrogen content to estimate maintenance respiration.

Prospective Method(s) and Frequency of Measurement: Ecosystem biomass components include living and dead fractions as well as above- and below-ground components. Obviously, the above-ground living component is the simplest to measure, while below-ground biomass (both living and dead) is very difficult to measure (Richter et.al.1999). Often, based on prior studies where total biomass has been measured, the relationship of below-ground to above-ground biomass is established and this relationship is used to predict below-ground amounts from above-ground measurements. Therefore, the method of monitoring involves the establishment of plots (often in the 0.05 ha [0.12 ac] size range) in which above-ground living biomass is measured. In actuality, biomass (dry weight) is seldom measured directly. Rather, biomass is estimated from easily measured attributes of the plants present (diameter, height, species, etc.). The above-ground component of dead biomass (leaf litter, dead wood, etc.) is also relatively measurable, but as with living biomass, the below-ground fraction of dead biomass is frequently estimated. Plots should be revisited on a five- to ten-year cycle in order to establish trends in biomass accumulation. An alternative to field measurements is to use remotely-sensed information to predict biomass. Satellite imagery has been used to develop the "Normalized Difference Vegetation Index (NDVI) and the Enhanced Vegetation Index (EVI). Such tools can be effective in differentiating between broad biomes (desert, savannah, deciduous forest, coniferous forest), and they are also effective at detecting large-scale drought stress within a biome. But at the level of the ERMN parks, they may be of limited value.

Limitations of Data and Monitoring: In order to monitor the state of biomass accumulation in a forested ecosystem, an extensive network of plots will be required. These will be expensive and difficult to install. Furthermore, in order to track biomass trends, these plots will need to be monitored every five to ten years. This requires that permanent plots be put in place, and the same plots should be measured periodically, which presents problems such as relocating the plots. The limitations with regard to the difficulty of sampling components such as below-ground biomass have been described above, and this and similar sampling problems necessitates the use of estimated values for non-measurable components. Therefore, to the extent that these estimates deviate from the actual values, errors will be made.

Key References:
Botkin, D. B., Janak, J. F. and Wallis, J. R. 1972. Some Ecological consequences of a computer model on forest growth. J. Ecol. 60:849-872.

Brinson, M. M., A. E. Lugo, and S. Brown. 1981. Primary productivity, decomposition, and consumer activity in freshwater wetlands. Annual Review of Ecology and Systematics 12:123-161.

Cairns, M. A., S. Brown, E. H. Helmer, and G. A. Baumgardner. 1997. Root biomass allocation in the world's upland forests. Oecologia 111(1):1-11.

DeLucia, E. H., and R. B. Thomas. 2000. Photosynthetic responses to CO_2 enrichment of four hardwood species in a forest understory. Oecologia 122:11-19.

Fahey, T. J., G. L. Tierney, R. D. Fitzburgh, G. F. Wilson, and T. G. Siccama. 2005. Soil respiration and soil carbon balance in a northern hardwood forest ecosystem. Canadian Journal of Forest Research 35(2):244-253.

Frank, P. S., Jr., R. R. Hicks, Jr., and E. J. Harner, Jr. 1984. Biomass predicted by soil-site factors: A case study in north central West Virginia. *Can. J. For. Res.* 14:137-140.

Geiger, R. J., E. H. DeLucia, P. G. Falkowski, A. C. Finzi, J. P. Grime, J. Grace, T. M. Kana, J. La Roche, S. P. Long, B. A. Osborne, and others. 2001. Primary productivity of planet earth: biological determinants and physical constraints in terrestrial and aquatic habitats. Global Change Biology 7:849-882.

Hamilton, J. G., R. B. Thomas, and E. H. Delucia. 2001. Direct and indirect effects of elevated CO2 on leaf respiration in a forest ecosystem. Plant, Cell and Environment 24:975-982.

Hicks, R. R., Jr. 1998. Ecology and Management of Central Hardwood Forests. John Wiley and Sons. New York, NY. 412 pp.

Mickler, R. A., T. S. Earnhardt, and J. A. Moore. 2002. Regional estimation of current and future forest biomass. Environmental Pollution 116:S7-S16.

Richter, D. D., D. Markewitz, S. E. Trumbore, and C. G. Wells. 1999. Rapid accumulation and turnover of soil carbon in a re-establishing forest. Nature 400:56-58.

Running, S. W., and S. T. Gower. 1991. Forest-BGC, a general model of forest ecosystem processes for regional applications, II. Dynamic carbon allocation and nitrogen budgets. Tree Physiology 9:147-160.

Ryan, M. G. 1991. A simple method for estimating gross carbon budgets for vegetation in forest ecosystems. Tree Physiology 9:255-266.

Weier, J., and D. Herring. 2005. Measuring Vegetation (NDVI & EVI). At http://earthobservatory.nasa.gov

Wharton, E. H., and G. K. Raile. 1984. Biomass statistics for the northern United States. USDA, Forest Service. Northeast Forest Exp. Sta. Res. Note NE-318. 3 p.

Related Environmental Issues and Linked Vital Signs: Primary productivity provides the energy that sustains all heterotrophic organisms in an ecosystem, and, given certain constraints, is an indicator of ecosystem health. Net Primary Production (NPP) is a function of the available resources and the stage of ecosystem development. NPP is linked to a wide array of other vital signs. For example, air pollutants (VS1, VS2) can reduce NPP, and weather, especially precipitation and temperature (VS4), can cause dramatic year-to-year fluctuations in NPP. Atmospheric enrichment with CO_2 can potentially increase biomass productivity by stimulating more rapid rates of photosynthesis (DeLucia and Thomas 2000). Geology and soils (VS11) are important in determining the productive potential of sites. Different forest plant communities (VS20) are inherently different in their productive potential, and anthropogenic impacts (VS54) can alter these communities, for example, by the introduction of invasive species (VS18) or via soil compaction. A number of animal species depend, either directly or indirectly, on the biomass from NPP, including birds (VS29, VS32), riparian mammals (VS30), invertebrates (VS34), white-tailed deer (VS38), and reptiles and amphibians (VS48). Finally, primary productivity is very important in processes such as decomposition and nutrient dynamics (VS60, VS61).

Overall Assessment: Because primary production of an ecosystem is the foundation of its trophic structure, and because it is linked to a variety of ecosystem attributes and functions, it is important to monitor trends in NPP in ERMN parks and to determine if biomass productivity is occurring within expected norms for healthy ecosystems. The field methodology for monitoring bio-productivity, however, is difficult and time consuming, especially with respect to below-ground components. But, because bio-productivity can affect many ecosystem properties, it may be worthwhile to monitor, if only on a relatively long-term measurement cycle (e.g. ten years).

Level 1 ▶ Ecosystem Pattern and Process
    Level 2 ▶ Nutrient Dynamics
        Level 3 ▶ Nutrient Dynamics (VS61)

Brief Description: "Nutrient Dynamics" involves the cycling of mineral nutrients through the soil-plant-water system as well as the inputs (atmospheric, rock weathering) and outputs, (leaching, stream export, aerosols, harvesting). A number of mineral substances are required for plant growth and development. A partial list of these includes the so-called "major nutrients" (nitrogen, phosphorous, potassium, magnesium, calcium and sulphur) as well as the "minor nutrients" (iron, copper, zinc, molybdenum, silicone, etc). These minerals are required as chemical reagents or co-factors in metabolic reactions; therefore, plants cannot survive without them. Nutrient dynamics involves processes such as wet and dry deposition, leaching, rock weathering, decomposition, mineralization, and plant uptake. Ecosystems are generally open systems with both inputs and outputs, but in order to maintain stability, these must achieve a balance. Nutrient dynamics is a fundamental ecosystem process, and as such, it can have broad-ranging effects on other processes such as primary productivity, forest health, and regeneration.

Significance/Justification: Nutrient dynamics, involving recycling of elements from organic residues as well as inputs and outputs, is subject to impacts from a variety of sources. For example, elevated deposition of nitrogen was found by Berg and Matzner (1997) to accelerate the rate of decomposition of newly fallen litter, but it slowed the rate of decomposition of later-stage humus. Acid deposition may increase the rate of mineral leaching, especially for base cations. Changes in forest systems, either as a result of changing land use (Currie and Nadelhoffer 2002), from timber harvesting (Patric and Smith 1975; Swank and Waide 1980), or loss of a species due to introduced insects or diseases (Yorks et al. 2004), can result in impacts to the nutrient balance. ERMN parks are exposed to many stressors, both from outside and from within. Maintaining healthy ecosystems involves the maintenance of healthy ecosystem processes and nutrient dynamics is one of the key processes that must be preserved.

Proposed Metrics: Nutrient capitol is often partitioned into pools (living biomass, dead biomass, mineral soil, etc.) and quantified as weight per mineral per unit bimass (mg/kg) or weight per area (kg/ha). When minerals are dissolved in water they are usually expressed in units like mg/l or parts per million. For mineral export in streams, loss is expressed as a rate function such as kg/ha/year.

Prospective Method(s) and Frequency of Measurement: In order to establish current levels of mineral nutrients in ERMN park ecosystems, a comprehensive analysis of living and dead biomass will be required. This would involve mass spectral analysis of mineral matter and chemical analysis of organic fractions; furthermore, these operations would have to be replicated in each ecosystem type at each park. It would also be desirable to monitor the key processes involved in nutrient dynamics (leaching, precipitation input, litter decomposition, stream export, mineralization, fixation, weathering, etc.). Methods are available to monitor some of these processes (Mudrick et al. 1994), but such undertakings would be very expensive. A more practical approach would be to monitor the inputs and outputs using the small watershed method (Federer et.al. 1990). This method involves measuring inputs by analyzing minerals deposited in precipitation and dry atmospheric deposition and output from stream flow. For the latter, the volume of water flowing from the watershed is measured at a control point using a weir. The difference between nutrient input and output indicates whether or not the system is in relative balance. Furthermore, tracking these parameters over time permits the observer to see whether or not the ratios of inputs and outputs remain constant or are changing.

Limitations of Data and Monitoring: Developing a viable system for monitoring nutrient dynamics, even using the small watershed approach, may be too difficult and expensive to conduct systemwide, therefore, perhaps one or a few watersheds could be instrumented in key parks. However, making the assumption that one or a few small watersheds can be representative of the larger whole is tentative at best, since even adjacent watersheds can produce dramatically different responses (Hicks 1992). Prediction models may be useful in estimating certain watershed parameters, for example, using readily-available precipitation data to estimate stream flows. But even here, some mechanism for calibrating and validating model projections is needed, usually involving the collection of field data.

Key References:

Berg, B., and E. Matzner. 1997. Effect of N deposition on decomposition of plant litter and soil organic matter in forest systems. Environ. Rev. 5(1):1-25.

Chadwick, O. A., L. A. Derry, P. M. Vitousek, B. J. Huebert, and L. O. Hedin. 1999. Changing sources of nutrients during four million years of ecosystem development. Nature 397:491-497.

Currie, W. S., and K. J. Nadelhoffer. 2002. The imprint of land-use history: patterns of carbon and nitrogen in downed woody debris at the Harvard Forest. Ecosystems 5(5):446-460.

Fassnacht, K. S., and S. T. Gower. 1999. Comparison of the litterfall and forest floor organic matter and nitrogen dynamics of upland forest forest ecosystems in north central Wisconsin. Biogeochemistry 45(3):265-284.

Federer, A. C., L. D. Flynn, C. W. Martin, J. W. Hornbeck, and R. S. Pierce. 1990. Thirty years of hydrometerologic study at the Hubbard Brook Experimental Forest, New Hampshire. USDA, Forest Service Gen. Tech. Rep. NE-144. 44 pp.

Hicks, R. R., Jr. 1992. Nutrient fluxes for two small watersheds: Seven-year results from the West Virginia University Forest. WV Agr. For. Exp. Sta. Bull. NO. 707. 29 pp.

Jones, K. B, A. C. Neale, M. S. Nash, R. D. Van Remortel, J. D. Wickham, K. H. Riitters, and R. V. O'Neill. 2001. Predicting nutrient and sediment loadings to streams from landscape metrics: a multiple watershed study from the United States Mid-Atlantic Region. Landscape Ecology 16:301-312.

King, J. S., H. L. Allen, P. Dougherty, and B. R. Strain. 1997. Decomposition of roots in loblolly pine: effects of nutrient and water availability and root size on mass loss and nutrient dynamics. Plant and Soil 195(1):171-184.

Krankina, O. N., M. E. Harmon, and A. V. Griazkin. 1999. Nutrient stores and dynamics of woody detritus in a boreal forest: modeling potential implications at the stand level. Canadian Journal of Forest Research 29(1):20-32.

Kraus, T. E. C., R. A. Dahlgren, and R. J. Zasoski. 2003. Tannins in nutrient dynamics of forest ecosystems: a review. Plant and Soil 256:41-66.

Mudrick, D. A., M. Hoosein, R. R. Hicks, Jr., and E. Townsend. 1994. Decomposition of leaf litter in an Appalachian Forest: Effects of leaf species, aspect, slope position, and time. *For. Ecol. and Mgt.* 68:231-250.

Patric, J. H., and D. W. Smith. 1975. Forest management and nutrient cycling in eastern hardwoods. USDA, Forest Servics. Res. Pap. NE-324. 12 p.

Swank, W. T., and J. T. Waide. 1980. Interpretimg nutrient cycling in a management context: Evaluating potential effects of alternative management strategies on site productivity. *In* Forests: Fresh Perspectives for Ecosystem Analysis. Proc. 40th Ann. Biol. Colloq. Oregon State University Press. 137-157.

Vose, J. M., C. Geron, J. Walker, and K. Raulund-Rasmussen. 2004. Chapter 5: Restoration effects on N cycling pools and processes. *In* Stanturf, J.A. & Madsen, P. (eds.), Restoration of Boreal and Temperate Forests. Pp. 500. CRC Press.

Yin, X. 1999. The decay of forest woody debris: numerical modeling and implications based on some 300 data cases from North America. Oecologia 121(1):81-98.

Yorks, T. E., J. C. Jenkings, D. J. Leopold, D. J. Raynal, and D. A. Orwig. 2004. Influences of Eastern Hemlock Mortality on Nutrient Cycling. USDA Forest Service, Proceedings: Symposium on Sustainable Management of Eastern Hemlock Ecosystems in Eastern North America, Gen. Tech. Rep. GTR-NE-267.

Related Environmental Issues and Linked Vital Signs: Mineral nutrients are primary resources required for the physiological functioning of all organisms within an ecosystem. The dynamics of these substances can alter the long-term health and productivity of the ecosystem. Many of the vital signs are linked with mineral nutrients. These include atmospheric and climatic factors (VS2, VS4). The soil and geologic material is one of the media through which processes such as plant uptake, leaching, and mineralization take place (VS12). Groundwater hydrology (VS15) plays a role in nutrient dynamics in that leached elements may find their way to deep storage pools in ground water. Communities (VS20, VS58), through litter production and decomposition (VS26, VS60), have an important effect on nutrient dynamics. And in the final analysis, nutrient dynamics is one of the drivers of primary productivity (VS59).

Overall Assessment: Nutrient dynamics describe the complex processes involving climatic, hydrologic, and biotic processes. Since minerals are required by all plants and animals in the ecosystem, the nutrient status has a profound effect on the health and productivity of the organisms. But monitoring nutrient dynamics at the ERMN park level will be difficult and expensive, necessitating the use of available data and modeling methods in lieu of field-based monitoring. Perhaps a reasonable compromise would include the addition of a limited number of small reference watersheds in key locations. Data collected from these watersheds could be used to calibrate modeling projections.

NPS D-025 July 2006